Wonderstruck
by **The Methow**

Other Books by Greg Wright

Tolkien in Perspective
Peter Jackson in Perspective
Two Roads Through Narnia
A Narnia Glossary of Obscure Terms
The Da Vinci Code Adventure
West of the Gospel
The Gospel of Doubt
What I Want for You

Wonderstruck
Wonderstruck by Art & Artists

Wonderstruck
by The Methow

**because the universe wants us to be in awe
of what comes next**

Greg Wright

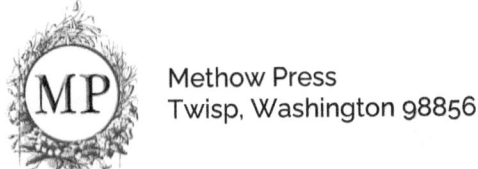

Methow Press
Twisp, Washington 98856

© 2018-2025 by Greg Wright

Published by Methow Press
P.O. Box 1213, Twisp, WA 98856
www.methowpress.com

Printed in the United States of America

All rights reserved. No part of this publication may be reproduced, stored in a retrieval system, or transmitted in any form or by any means—for example, electronic, photocopy, or recording—without the prior written permission of the publisher. The only exception is brief quotations in printed reviews.

Essays in this work have appeared previously on Facebook and Medium.

ISBN: 979-8-9913567-4-9

Cover image courtesy NASA.

Unless otherwise noted, all Scripture quotations in this work are from The Holy Bible, New International Version ® NIV ® Copyright © 1973, 1978, 1984 by the International Bible Society. All rights reserved.

Extended quotes from books, songs, and poetry written by the author's friends and associates have been used by permission. Other quotes from works by public figures are used under Fair Use provisions of U.S. copyright law and are intended, as a form of scholarly critique, to draw attention to and praise the works of those public figures.

Contents

Introduction	i
Falls Creek	1
The West	5
Sherry Malotte	8
Subhaga Crystal Bacon	10
Jason Suter	13
Skalitude	17
The Barnyard	19
Nicole Ringgold	21
Dragonflies	22
Terry L. Pisel	24
Harmony	27
Robin Doggett	30
Cindy Williams Gutiérrez	33
Sourdoug	37
Jesse Tissell	39
Community	41
Erika Lundahl	45
Appointments	50
Norman Baker	52
Aging	54
Shannon Huffman Polson	57
Pressure	60
Theater	63
Casting	67
Ian Maclaren	71
Jennifer Epps	74
A Coen Dream	77
Cristofori's Dream	80
Westendorf	84
Authenticity	87
Cello… and Poetry	91
Mountainfilm	94
Maracci	98
Crispy Bats	102
Varn	105
Sacrifice	108
Zoe	112
Pelotonia	116
Shekels	119
Pirateer	123
Bullion	127
Kaileah Akker	130
Epona Rose	135
Panties	138
The Methow	142
Lost & Found	146
Lolita in Tehran	152
Meza	156
Deadfall	158
Thingol and Melian	161
Leen	167
Beast Mode	170
In Memory Of	173
Nobacon	179
Early Winters	182
Methow's Bombadil	185
Acknowledgements	191

Introduction

After my wife, Jenn, passed away at the end of 2017 in the wake of nearly fifteen years of terminal illness, I began writing a series of letters to her on a Facebook page titled "Memos to the Missus." The tagline was "Because who else would I tell?"

From that grew the first Wonderstruck essay, an exceedingly simple reflection on my April 2018 raft trip through the Grand Canyon and a performance of Ferde Grofé's "Grand Canyon Suite" by the Auburn, Washington, Symphony—an unexpected treat as part of a musical program co-hosted by performance artist and friend Adrian Wyard.

The essays which followed have been predicated on a profound belief that life is not entirely random… and that the intention of the universal and infinite works itself out through the interactions that we have with one another and all the world around us.

Hence my belief that serendipity brought me to the Methow. When people ask how I came to live in this valley, the short answer is: God picked me up by the scruff of the neck and plopped me here.

The longer, if still incomplete, answer is: *Wonderstruck*, the collection of essays which explains my journey of grief and healing from a philosophical and metaphysical point of view.

The collection of essays you now hold, however, is specifically about some of the people, places, and experience of the Methow which fill me with awe and wonder. And I really do believe the universe guided many of the interactions here recorded.

Everything that you read in these pages is 100% true, if much of it wildly improbable. I have lived my questions, as Rilke once recommended to a young poet, and these essays are a record of my progress, gradually, without perhaps even noticing it, toward living into my own answers.

I invite you to question my experience, to ponder whether such a universe can actually exist.

But be patient with my words, especially if they resonate, and read them slowly. And also be patient with your own journey as you live your own questions in this very, very surprising universe.

Greg Wright
Winthrop, Washington
December 1, 2024

Falls Creek

"A force of nature" is a description that I have found apt of a great many people, but upon reflection on remarks that young Ria Montenegro made in a banquet speech the other night, I think it's fair to say that the most empowered people are not those who become "forces of nature" in their own right, but those who align themselves with the forces of nature around them.

That makes sense, right? After all, which is more powerful: you, or Snoqualmie Falls? You, or the winds that shape Cape Flattery? You, or the wonder of conception and gestation which formed you? You won't get far if you are constantly fighting the flow, if you insist on "kicking at the goads," as it were.

I met Ria at a scholarship awards banquet last Wednesday. Back in the day, I was blessed enough to myself be a four-year recipient of a Nellie Martin Carman Scholarship Fund award. Like Ria, the only reason I was in the running in the first place was because a school counselor had said, "You know, you ought to consider submitting an application for this scholarship…"

As an alumnus of the scholarship program, I had been asked to deliver the "keynote" address to conclude the evening's program; but I believe that the most powerful speech delivered that night was Ria's.

She spoke just before me, and the just-graduated math major talked about the many times that unexpected opportunities came her way—and how she has consistently listened to the still, small voice within her that has said, "Yes! You should not just consider taking advantage of this opportunity; you need to jump at the chance and follow through. What do you have to lose, when you have so much to gain?"

Ria's summation: If someone ever introduces an opportunity to you with the words, "You might consider...," pay attention! This is the Universe talking to you, because that's the way the Universe works. And because it so deeply wants us to get on board with its agenda, it often uses people and forces outside our own small selves to guide and direct us.

I was only listening to Ria's speech, of course, because scholarship administrator Sheri Baer Ashleman had said to Ria and other recent graduates, "Would you consider offering a few words of wisdom to undergraduates at this year's banquet?"

I was thinking about Ria's words quite a bit over the last weekend, particularly as I was exploring the Falls Creek trail near Winthrop.

I had come to the Methow for music, but it really wasn't working for me. Instead, I asked the attendant at Big Twin Lake Campground for a trail recommendation.

And so, early Saturday afternoon, I was steaming steeply uphill in temperatures above 90 degrees, and the grade showed no signs of lessening. From the online description, I knew that at 1.25 miles I had already passed the visual highlight of the trail, the uppermost of four waterfalls; but another half mile of sweltering elevation gain remained before the trail would level out. On this stretch, you couldn't even see the creek. Was it worth the heat?

I thought of Ria's words. Here was an opportunity that would not likely present itself to me again. What were the odds that I would be on this trail another time? Would the conditions likely be any better? Would my own condition likely be any better?

Is there any guarantee that any other trail would be better on another day?

The energy I had already put into the hike had been well rewarded. This was a good trail, a most excellent trail, a demanding and rewarding trail.

I remembered that the Big Twin Lake attendant had rattled off some rather conventional trail recommendations before he sized me up and said, "You really ought to consider the Falls Creek trail..." Hmm...

So yes, I decided, it was worth the heat.

I felt great. At 1.75 miles, the trail does level out before descending sharply to its end at 2.0 miles and a forest road.

I eyed the last few hundred yards of trail and thought, "Do I want to go down there? I'll just be turning around, and then I have to gain that elevation back immediately. It's so hot!" But I thought about Ria's words again, and down I went.

When would ever I be on this trail again?

Where the Falls Creek trail terminates at the forest road, it finally comes right alongside the placid stream bank. A small sandy beach abuts a waist-deep pool of clear, cold water in the full overhead sun. A quick, cooling dip in Falls Creek beckoned. How inconvenient it would be... to have to dry and clean my sandy feet and all before rebooting... yeah.

And I thought again of Ria's words. I bet you can guess what I decided.

What do you have to lose, when you have so much to gain?

■

The West

I could have titled this, "Wonderstruck by Books... because the universe wants us to confess to traitorous behavior." But I don't care to be so up front with my confession.

Thirty years ago I was shooting a Western film in the Okanogan. This summer, because my first impressions of the Methow Valley were so strong and serendipitous, I am completing steps to sell my suburban Puget Sound home and buy a house in Twisp.

Today I succumbed to the very bad news of very real math and decided that I can no longer pay to store books that I intend to sell at some point in the future to the highest bidder on eBay. Because the more time that passes, the more money I am losing on the delayed transaction. Sure, there are other things besides books in my storage locker... but those have little market value.

Those boxes of treasured books, however...

I confessed to the manager at Half Price Books this morning that I was indeed conflicted about letting go of so many of my collectible tomes at a fraction of their value. It was almost worse than taking Grynne and Bearrett back to the cat rescue shelter from whence they came after a decade in the homes which my recently-deceased wife, Jenn, and I made with the four of us!

I dare not offend my bookish friends by detailing all the books I let go of today, but suffice to say that a good many of them were volumes that I literally lived with from 1986 through 2010—the years I was working on my film *Who Shall Stand*, my novel *West of the Gospel*, and their companion stories.

Gone now are a first edition of Ramon Adams' *Western Words*, Ruby El Hult's *The Big Blowup*, John G. Bourke's *On the Border with Crook*, and the official history of the all-Black 25th Regiment of the U.S. Infantry.

And, yes, all my Charles M. Russells. It almost makes me cry.

No, wait. It *does* make me cry.

I first saw Russell's work in the coffee-table book *Trails Plowed Under*, which was a gift from my grandmother to my mom and dad sometime in the 1960s. She may have purchased it for them from the Russell Museum in Great Falls when we lived there in 1967.

Russell's work depicts the vanishing West as it had been known in the nineteenth century; although Russell came along toward the end of the century, he was a good listener and worked the range with many an old-timer who had seen firsthand the things that Russell drew and painted.

When I began work on *Who Shall Stand*, I tracked down and purchased (rare) copies of everything that Russell published during his lifetime.

My most treasured find was a copy of *Rawhide Rawlins Stories*.

Here's a sample of Rawhide's lingo, his description of falling asleep while on horseback:

> From feelin' musical I begin to get sleepy, and the last I remember I'm dozin' off. I recollect Bill reachin' for the reins, and the next I know I've a vague notion I'm in an airship and can see clear to the Mexican line. I'm wonderin' where I changed cars when the light goes out.

Russell's ear for the vernacular completely informed the flavor of dialogue in my film and novel. His books, and the others in my Western collection (including the vast ghost town catalogs), will always be in my mind and in my heart.

There I go tearing up again. Dang it!

So why am I cuttin' 'em out the herd? Cause I can't hold on to ever'thin', not fer ever. Leastwise in the case of the Westerns... well, I don't need to study them no more. Nor write no more stories nor shoot movin' pitchers about 'em. Nope.

I'll be *livin'* it, pardner.

■

Sherry Malotte

The first person I struck up a conversation with during my first walk in Twisp was photographer Sherry Malotte.

Sherry shares studio space in Twispworks with illustrator Hannah Viano. My second conversation was with Hannah, who recently got a chance to do her work for a time in the Shetlands. How cool is that? Hannah's woodblock prints are really striking.

Twispworks itself is a pretty awe-inspiring "discovery," if one can discover something so public. As the website notes, "Campus partners include businesses, artists, community services and educational programs. All share a strong drive to create, thrive and connect. Together, they form a magical environment where ideas and collaborations flow and evolve."

As you might imagine, it was one of the things that appealed to me about Twisp. Sealed the deal, if you will, when my local real estate agent, Kathy Curtiss, drove me around town while we toured properties.

I was walking over to the Saturday Twisp Farmers' Market when I decided to tour the Twispworks campus. Connecting with Sherry's photography was pretty natural, of course—particularly one of her preferred media, metal prints. If you haven't heard of that medium before, it's very well described by trademarked processor MetalPrints: "an art medium for preserving photos by infusing dyes directly into specially coated aluminum sheets. Your images will take on a magical luminescence." So very true.

After Jenn went on hospice care last fall, I ordered a metalprint triptych of one of her shots of the Icicle Creek valley outside Leavenworth. It's a blue and white eyeful, with the various cerulean shades popping out with startling luminosity.

Sherry's work is full of this luminescence. I was particularly drawn to her abstract studies of fallen leaves, which reminded me a great deal of some of Jenn's work. We talked about the difference of effect between wider, clearer shots and tighter, blurred shots.

Her website says:

> I am passionate about my abstract work, as it allows me to explore concepts and emotions in art that evoke a sense of wonder about the subject matter. The idea of beauty is always with me when I am creating. My purpose is to provide as much beauty for the world that I can possibly muster!

Purpose fulfilled, sister. Purpose fulfilled!

■

Subhaga Crystal Bacon

I walked over to attend "Reflections on Water" at Confluence Gallery in Twisp last evening.

For ninety minutes, Methow Valley members of the Confluence Poets read selections "inspired by all things water." Many of the readings were connected to works displayed in the mixed-media "Reflections on Water" art exhibit in the Confluence Main Gallery.

"Living in the Methow Valley creates an awareness of water beyond turning on a tap or quenching thirst; water here is a way of life," says Christine Kendall of the Confluence Poets, who emceed and read. "We also know the beauty of water in all its many forms, and just as poets have done for centuries we will celebrate it in our writing."

Boy howdy.

Confluence Poets is not your typical local writers' group. Twisp is a hub of artistic productivity, and many of the active CP members have very long CVs and publishing histories.

One of those who read last night was Subhaga Crystal Bacon. I particularly loved her poem "Invitation," the opening lines of which I include below. You can read it in full on her blog.

I picked up a volume of 2004's *Elegy with a Glass of Whiskey* (published under her birth-name, Crystal) during the intermission last night, and then Googled her when I returned home. Subhaga is not only a fine poet who thinks well about both her words and their oral delivery; she is also a brilliant essayist who is on a committed journey of discovery and awakening.

Here are some samples of her writing.

> We all have our wounds, our fears, our feelings of worthlessness. Poets have written this over and over across the eons. We have to open the door, me, then you, then me, then you, over and over and over again until the light of our love illuminates the dark corners, and we know ourselves loved.

■

> Life is a beautiful and horrifying venture. We are typically born in blood and pain, and we are likely to die in it as well. Along the way are poignant stops that bring us great blessings and joys and then the unfathomable grief of their loss. We must allow ourselves to live the full spectrum of this truth. Anything else is a lie, and we will leave this body and the life it has either enjoyed or endured without having known our full potential, without having known God, Love, Truth. Whatever we call it, the only way to know it is to let ourselves descend fully into each experience, to make room for it, to live it to the fullest of our ability. This is the path to wisdom; this is the path to living a life in and as consciousness in whole Being realization. This is the path to awakened life.

■

Everyone's awakening is different. Everyone's conditioning is different. The shell that separates us from our true nature may be more or less dense depending on a multitude of factors. But once we catalyze the process, we can be sure that it will take us with it to the eventuality of a deep knowing of all that we are. If you're reading this, then you may already be in its embrace. Maybe you are one with it, and maybe you are wrestling. But you know its hold, and you can be sure that it is not going to let go.

■

When you are ready,
come. I will be waiting
by the river's
purling hurry,
slim or sleek
with spring.
We will walk there
and your story–
river in ice,
river hurling–
will quicken.

■

Jason Suter

I landed on Burton Street in Twisp by the real estate equivalent of throwing darts at a map.

Yet the chain of coincidence is stacking up like a plateful of Providence.

When I first drove into Twisp on Friday, July 20, 2018, I was on a very particular mission. I wanted to connect with a handcrafted jewelry specialist while I was on vacation, and had Googled Nicole Ringgold Jewelry Designs by searching for silversmiths in the Methow. By connecting with her on Facebook I learned that her workspace was in the back of garden shop Yard Food at the corner of Highway 20 and Burton Street. I dropped in while Nicole was conducting a workshop with five or six students, including her daughter. I saw such wonderful work from them all!

That visit was part of an entire four days of serendipity, which I wrote about during a stop at Alta Lake on my drive home that Sunday.

Later in that drive, I got to thinking about my home in Des Moines. It had been for sale almost three months at that point, with nary a nibble—so taking it off the market might make sense. After all, I had no idea where I would live if my house sold! I had no plans and felt no specific guidance from God; I just very strongly felt the need to move… or at least the need to be prepared to move.

Driving through the Swauk Prairie south of Blewett Pass, however, awoke within me a long-suppressed desire to live east of the Cascades. I have always loved the Swauk and Teanaway valleys and had even talked about the Teanaway with new friend Eric Peterson at Sun Mountain Lodge the previous evening.

That spurred me to do some browsing on Zillow when I got home. Prices in the Teanaway were too inflated for my taste, as it turned out. But I thought: Well, what about the Methow? I had seen a couple of super homes for sale along Highway 153 on my drive that day.

A few houses looked like possibilities; but one in Twisp just popped out at me. My heart said, "Greg, that's the house you need to buy." 906 Burton Street. Wow, I thought. That's got to be right down the street from Yard Food.

Yep. Sure enough. What a coincidence!

But then my heart sank. The house was so perfect, there's no way it would stay on the market long enough for my own house to sell. No way. I went to bed Sunday night stoked by new possibilities but pretty bummed that I was probably going to miss out.

When I sat down at my computer Monday morning, the first thing I checked was my email account, and the first email in my inbox was *an offer on my house*.

That was exactly two months ago. As you might imagine, given that I've been living in Twisp for more than a week now, the necessary dominoes starting falling the very morning of July 23. Everything happened exactly as it needed for me to close the sale of my Des Moines home... including an unexpected text from my real estate agent while I was camped with The Shy Pilot on a trackless ledge in the Alpine Lakes Wilderness... when there was no reason for my cell phone to be on... where cell coverage shouldn't have even been possible... and when an urgent piece of paperwork needed completion!

The sale of my Des Moines home closed September 12 and the purchase of my Burton Street house closed September 14.

On Saturday September 15, with my brand new NCI Datacom Internet connection on Burton Street, I Googled the possibilities for churches to attend the next day. Even though Cascade Bible Church is right there on Highway 20 at the head of Burton Street, something inside me told me that Friendship Alliance Church in Winthrop was the place to be.

During my first visit the next day, I met George and Candy North Hoksbergen and pastor Jason Suter, among other folks, as well as Terry L. Pisel—another transplant to the Methow who was also visiting FAC for the first time. Terry and I sat in the same row and pretty instantly struck up a friendship.

On Thursday, I had lunch with Terry and then messaged Jason when I got home, mentioning that I'd like to talk with him further about his own intriguing journey from Ohio to the Methow.

I saw in Jason's Facebook profile that he also lives in Twisp. *Wow*, thought I. *It sure will be easy to get together with Jason for lunch.*

On the drive to church yesterday morning, the thought occurred to me: *Wouldn't it be funny if it turned out that Jason and his family lived on Burton Street somewhere?*

Twisp isn't that big of a town, after all. And in all honesty, I have long dreamed of having a close, neighborly relationship with a pastor.

The first person I met when I arrived at church yesterday morning was Jason's wife, Katie. After we exchanged introductions, she looked at me quizzically and said, "I recognize you. Didn't you just move in on Burton Street in Twisp?"

Jason and Katie and their children live on the other side of my backyard fence on Burton Street. Katie and I had waved hello to each other a couple of times during the week without realizing who the other was.

Small town? Small Universe.

Big God.

■

Skalitude

I stumbled across Skalitude Eco-Retreat while on a drive yesterday.

This off-the-grid education and retreat center is tucked at the end of Smith Canyon Road outside Carlton and is "a sanctuary dedicated to being in harmony with nature." In addition to hosting retreats and weddings, the goal of Skalitude is to "provide education on sustainable living practices" via hands-on programs and experience "lodging in our solar-powered Lodge and Bermhouse."

The facility is managed by Maeyoka Grace Brightheart, and one of its projects is establishing a honey bee sanctuary—which fits right in with its more general goal of providing sanctuary, solitude, and silence for human beings who need to reconnect with nature. Skalitude's spiritual inspiration is drawn from many sources, including "shamanism, Findhorn (Scotland), Perelandra (Virginia) and Celtic traditions."

If Perelandra sounds familiar, that's the name of a C.S. Lewis novel, from which Machelle Wright drew inspiration. I've visited the Findhorn community in Scotland and can vouch for the authenticity of that connection—which also inspired Wright. If all of this sounds really "out there"... yep. Skalitude is definitely end-of-the-road out there, like Findhorn and Perelandra... but that's really the point of being out there.

Everything's a little scary, when you think about it. Big cities aren't exactly safe, and even small towns have their issues.

Personally, I love the little surprises you find out at the end of the road. I liked this particular surprise well enough that I returned after dark last night to watch the new moon rise over the east ridge above Skalitude. As the sliver of silver inched its way into view, I was struck by realizing that, in all my years in the woods, I've never taken the time to simply watch the moon rise over a mountain top. I did last night. It was magical.

Later, as I was waiting for another thirty-second exposure to capture the Big Dipper over the west rim of Skalitude's pasture, I heard crackling in the thickets. For a few moments, I wondered if elk were going to make a foraging visit; but soon, in the moonlight, I could see the hulks of several cattle returning home from their grazing.

Yes, I stayed until the cows came home.

■

The Barnyard

Perhaps I am easily impressed.

On Saturday night I decided to check out the local theater in Winthrop and went to see *Crazy Rich Asians*. The Barnyard Cinema is a fifteen-minute traffic-free drive away for me and sits on the southern outskirts of Winthrop. It's a single-screen house and shows a double feature each night, with matinees on weekends. Says the website:

> Founded by three Methow Valley couples with wide-ranging skill sets and interests, the idea for The Barnyard Cinema hatched in April 2015. After more than two years of blood, sweat and tears (almost literal), a few bumps in the road, and the odd crisis of confidence, the cinema is open for business. As a friend expressed, "Six partners? You're all going to heaven."

I've gotta say... The Barnyard is pretty much cinema heaven.

Not to toot my own horn, because that's not at all what Wonderstruck is about, but I have screened films in a ton of moviehouses around the world, including Disney's private screening rooms, and even attended the Royal Premiere of *Voyage of the Dawn Treader* in London (that's the screening the Queen attends, in case you were wondering). And all I can say is that The Barnyard ought to host every press screening of every film. Reviews would easily be one star higher across the board. The quality of presentation is that good.

In addition to the game room and bar/lounge, The Barnyard features massive recliners for every seat on the main floorspace. Now, that's not all that unusual these days... but this is: instead of staring at endless promotional garbage while you wait for the movie to start, you gaze westward out The Barnyard's massive windows to the North Cascade peaks as the sun sets. A few minutes before showtime, the curtains close, you say goodbye to Mt. Gardner, and the screen descends. You are subjected to only a couple of trailers, and the show begins.

Projection? Perfect. Dolby surround audio? Oh. My. Gosh.

And you are sharing this with only fifty or so people. Hoodathunk?

Yeah, I'm gonna like my new home.

■

Nicole Ringgold

Nicole Ringgold Jewelry Designs was the first place I visited in Twisp. I specifically wanted to find a silversmith, and Nicole was actually conducting a workshop the week I was visiting town and invited me to drop in and observe for a bit. I was able to see works in progress from several students and even purchased a set of earrings from a first-timer!

What a twist of fate that the house the universe handed me turned out to be just down the street from Nicole's studio.

One of the things I learned about Nicole's work, which I love, is how she is inspired by the wonder that surrounds her. While out on walks and hikes in the neighboring hills, or while puttering in the garden, she will find feathers and cones and blossoms—even frogs in the kitchen!—whose shapes speak and call to her mind and fingers. How amazing are the skills that allow her to translate vision into silver reality!

And what a strange sense of contentment I get knowing that such artistry is available to me just one hundred yards from my front door.

There is so much such art here in Twisp. I feel like a kid in a town filled with candy shops!

■

Dragonflies

This one's for my sister, Elane…

As I was walking to the post office last evening to pick up my mail, I found twenty-one cents outside the Eagles Club.

Immediately afterward, I found a dying dragonfly in the middle of the sidewalk. I picked him up, and he fluttered his front wings weakly. Not knowing what to do with a dying dragonfly—uncharted waters for me here, as I'd never before held a living one, even a partly living one, in my hand—I elected to place him in a shrub by the sidewalk. I had errands to run. Maybe he'd still be there, alive, when I returned.

After stopping at the Eagles Club for a burger, I continued on to see if Cinnamon Twisp was still open. It was not. (It closes at 3 PM, which I should have known.) When I checked my mail, there was an $800 refund check from the escrow company handling my house purchase here in Twisp. Bonus! Every good deed, as they say.

On the way home, I checked the shrub by the sidewalk. Nearly an hour had passed, but there the dragonfly still was. I picked him up, and he settled into the palm of my hand for the ten-minute walk home. Upon reaching home, I shot some photographs of him and gave him some sugar water, not knowing what else to try. Then I took him outside to let nature take its course.

As I was walking the dragonfly home, I was very conscious of being excessively sensitive to insect life. I kind of wanted to encounter another walker to whom I could show the dragonfly... but was also a little afraid of being too easily identified as a Methow newbie. And a sentimental, artsy-fartsy one at that. *So be it*, I thought. *Wouldn't be the first time.*

The other afternoon when I was walking back from lunch with Jason Suter, I did the same thing with a dying "painted lady" butterfly—but it was still too lively to be okay with being held.

Will holding these beautiful insects in my hand get old?

Will I become jaded to dying butterflies and dragonflies?

■

Terry L. Pisel

Terry and I met at Winthrop Friendship Alliance Church a couple of weeks ago.

We were both visiting for the first time and sat in the same row, striking up easy conversation both before and after church.

Terry L. Pisel came to the Valley a year ago under circumstances not dissimilar to mine. Last week, he was on vacation in Idaho with his dog, Obi, enjoying places dear to both his and my hearts. What follows is his account of the sunset over Twisp upon his return Thursday night—and he has graciously allowed me to reprint it in full.

> Obi and I arrived back in the Methow Valley last night right at sunset. We were descending from the "Loup," as it's known locally, a pass over the mountains separating us from the Okanogan River Valley to the east, and were close to the bottom just as the sun set behind the North Cascade Mountains to the west.
>
> I try not to read too much into daily occurrences in my life, but the sunset that proceeded to unfold was nothing short of a spiritual sign and blessing confirming for me that I was indeed "home"! It's kind of funny, because wish as I could and try as I might, there was absolutely nowhere for me to pull off the road in the motor home to capture an image of

the more-than-incredible display. The two-lane highway is narrow, winding, shoulder-less, and busy most of the time.

So, as the miles went by and we drew near the small town of Twisp, the show unfolded for me in complete grandeur. Finally, in desperation, I squeezed to the side of the highway across from Burton St. in Twisp where my newly found friend and fellow recent arrival, Greg Wright, lives.

However, with a sigh of disappointment, I quickly realized that I was not only blocking highway traffic but had a view filled with power lines. No photo of this incredible display to share!

Coming from the Southwest and traveling as much as I have, I've seen amazing sunsets before, too many to count. I mean, come on, the Arizona state flag is a sunset! But this one was not like any of those past. Yes, it colored the clouds in reds and yellows and every color in between. It had shafts of light and shadows like the others. However, this one had shafts of bright sunlight cast through and around the high mountain peaks of the North Cascade Range back in the distance. The peak-shaped shafts of light were streaming through, lighting the lower mountains above the Methow Valley, casting shadows of the jagged, high mountain peaks through the sky. In the center of it all was the blazing fireball, extinguishing itself into a cleft between the high peaks.

I'll never forget the incredible beauty of that sunset and the reassurance I've found in it. Upon reflection, I came to the realization that the timing of my arrival, along with the exact place I was at the time, was set just for me, like a stage. It was meant for me, to express to me the fact that I am exactly where I am supposed to be at this exact time in my life. It wasn't meant to share as an image but rather as an experience, confirming that there is a time and a season for everything in life, for every one of us.

And it also confirms for me that I should often just let life unfold, forgetting about trying to capture it for some purpose other than what it is for… experiencing that exact time and place, just as God intended. Ecclesiastes 3:1-8

Yeah. Wonderstruck.

Harmony

"The words have worlds out at the edges of the shadow," writes poet and big-game skinner Harmony Cronin, "where you might never think to wander the grounds of the Hallowed."

Last night's Poetry Slam at Sixknot Organic Hard Cider, a benefit for Friends of The Winthrop Public Library, was most definitely an opportunity to step outside "the habit of the mouth," as Harmony describes our usual failure to "enter the language." For two hours, a dozen local poets and musicians regaled a full taproom with their "gnarled knobs of shift and change."

Joshua Dodds took first prize for the night, his deep-throated paean to the legacy of American bison proving a memorable highlight. There was so much to celebrate in the words of Molly H. Lachapelle, Epona Heathen, Eileen (Sam) Owen, Taylor Fulton, Ken Bevis, Rico Stover, Rachel Macmorran, and others whose names I fail to remember.

But I was floored by Harmony's "The Words Are Elders."

I had the chance to speak to Harmony between rounds of reading, and she lamented (as does her poem) the dearth of true elders in today's culture—sage, learned, and respected voices with the earned authority to remind you "of your own stark poverty" and challenge you to "walk callow and humbled" in "the footprints of the Makers."

Like me, and obviously like a great many others in this valley, Harmony often turns instead to words themselves for inspiration and solace.

> Bring a gift or a few
> And follow the tastes in the air
> With patience & learning you may find words still yearning
> To tell you their stories, their lives come to bear
> So fall on your knees at the seat of the spoken
> The battered faces wrinkled and open
> Let them pour forth their draught of the story
> Let them enchant you with what this culture has buried

Poets have a gift for using words in arresting ways to provoke thought and change. But Harmony was taking things one step further here, using the richness of language to talk about the magic of the poet's very toolset and anthropomorphize it.

She was gracious enough to give me the hand-written copy of "The Words" from which she had read, so that I could immerse myself in the text more thoroughly and write about the poem. It figured that she would be currently reading John McWhorter's *Our Magnificent Bastard Tongue: The Untold History of English*. I was also not surprised to learn that Harmony had studied *Beowulf* in Old English.

I have spent a great deal of time with Middle English texts myself and could sense that Harmony knows how to make words supple in the same way that she knows how to tan hides. It takes, first, a knowledge and appreciation of what's underneath, then a desire to slice through the blood and guts that others most often avoid, and finally the long patience to strip away the fat and flesh and outer grain to reveal what actually lies beneath. Work it and wring it for all you're worth, until the texture is just right.

But that's what poets do.

> You might yet learn something worthy
> Something unwelcome but trued
> From the busted-tooth Old Timers
> Unmannered and crude
> Sitting there in the smokelight
> In the shambles of anguish
> If you're wise enough, fool enough
> To enter the language

Wow.

I'm sitting here now picturing a night around the fire with my friends the ancient words. Because they are still so, so alive.

And that's what it felt like I did last night at Sixknot.

What a gift.

∎

Robin Doggett

> I'm driving down this highway
> Dandelion wishes float past
> Catching one last breath of summer
> Before she leaves and man she's going fast

As I was prepping to venture out the other night for the Twisp Sip 'n Chat business networking event, I put on a CD recorded by friends: Skybound Blue's album *Better Than the Plans We Made*. The song which follows the disc's title track is "Home Is Where Your Heart Is."

> The next time that you see me
> I'll be frozen, weathered and worn
> But I'll come gently if you'll have me
> Hold you close and never let you go

The album wraps up with a reprise of the song, and it was concluding just as I walked out the door.

> Trying to see beyond my headlights
> Pounding through this black night
> Farther from my home
> "Home is where your heart is."

The lyric was still running through my head as I walked into Robin Doggett's print shop in the 2nd Avenue alley west of Highway 20. She was hosting the Chamber of Commerce

"Sip 'n Chat" to celebrate her shop's opening. I arrived well after things had gotten underway and immediately sidled into the only available wallspace in the workshop.

On the wall in front of me were two brand-new batches of letterpressed Christmas cards.

The one on the left read, "Home is where the heart is."

If I had been sitting in a chair, I would have fallen out of it!

Yes, the phrase is common enough—but that song has meant so much to me over the last three months, and Twisp has been just a godsend. And timing ... well, you know how I feel about such things as that.

I didn't get a chance to talk much to Robin (or anyone else) that night before I had to step out to see a screening of *Dawn Wall* at The Barnyard. So I paid Robin another visit yesterday.

We talked at length about her work with letterpress printing and her past partnership with Laura Gunnip at Door No. 3 Print Studio at Twispworks. I met Laura during my first week in Twisp and had seen Robin's letterpress there, before she and her husband, Joe, moved it to the new shop space.

The letterpress is a 1911 model, a device of the type invented by Gutenberg. According to those who know, "letterpress printing is a form of relief printing, where the text or image is on a raised surface, similar to a rubber stamp. Ink is applied to the raised surface and then paper is pressed directly against it to transfer the text/image. ... Today, letterpress printing is loved by many for leaving a tactile and visual impression into the paper—some call it 'debossed.'"

Robin has used the method to print projects in collaboration with local artists like Hannah Viano, as well as custom promotional pieces for organizations such as the Methow Conservancy. I of course bought some of her Christmas cards!

Oh. And like me, Robin is a transplant from west of the Cascades.

In fact, she grew up in Federal Way on Dash Point Road, just south of where I used to live. Dash Point Road was part of my daily commute for many years.

Robin also graduated from Decatur High School just a couple years before my late wife, Jennifer Cram Wright. They were in concert band at the same time. Band nerds unite!

This place and the people I meet here just continue to amaze me.

Home is where your heart is. Oh, yeah.

■

Cindy Williams Gutiérrez

During a long drive from Seattle to Salem a year ago, I listened to the collected musical works of MaMuse, a mostly-acoustic Chico-based duo I've known since 2008.

I was thinking a lot about Jenn during that drive, not surprisingly, as it was my first road trip without her, and one song in particular leapt out at me. "You're Not Crazy."

> You were born of a wild wind
> Here to tear all the burdens down
> Start anew with your own hands
> Build it up from the very ground
>
> You were born with a strong will
> Equally matched by a warm heart
> Creative vision and a clear sight
> You knew your work from the very start
>
> Oh, You're not crazy
> You're not crazy
> You're not crazy
> You're just mad

I wept, naturally. That so described Jenn, right down to the double n.

I was amazed that I hadn't really heard those lyrics before. I probably hadn't wanted to, because the song concludes with this very hard truth: "Hey, remember we knew / It was gonna be this way / When we came."

Yes. Yes, we did.

We were not promised a bed of roses, as they say. We knew that our love would travel on a gravel road, as Elvis once sang.

> You have to forgive the stones that cut your feet

Cindy Williams Gutiérrez wrote those last words, and others which follow, in her poem "You have to go on," which she delivered to a meeting of the Confluence Poets on Wednesday afternoon.

I dislike gravel roads, and I particularly hate crossing them in bare feet, as those close to me would know. But sometimes there's only one way to get to the other side.

> You have to make your way around rocks like a river
> You have to climb each boulder with both hands

A year ago, I was starting to work through that "going on." After a few days in Salem, I drove up to Ocean Shores, the "scene of the crime," as it were: I ended up staying in exactly the same room that Jenn and I did when she came down catastrophically septic on Christmas Eve 2013. This time, on Christmas Day, my sister, Elane, and I took a long, windy walk down the spit at Damon Point. Along the way, she shared that she loved looking for heart-shaped stones while beachwalking. Damon Point is a superb place to look, as the beach is a solid mile and a half of small, polished stones.

As we walked, and as I thought, I picked out three heart-shaped stones for myself and pocketed them. And then forgot all about them.

As I was walking back from the post office in the snow on Tuesday this week, I stuck my hand in my pocket and was surprised to find rocks in it. I apparently had not worn my oilskin drover's coat for a year. I stopped and examined these hearts of stone in my hand.

Memory came rushing back.

As I crossed the Methow on the Twisp bridge, I paused and gazed into the clear water. The pebbles made barely noticeable splashes as they settled to their new bed. They'll stay there for a while and remind me of Jenn from time to time as I walk by.

Eventually the waters will take them on down this valley.

> You have to go on.
> You have to empty your pocket of pebbles

Tuesday and Wednesday mornings I was working on "Poesy," a piece about memory, inexpressibility, and dwelling with silence.

"You don't have to walk in a straight path / You don't have to run to catch your breath / You only have to sit when the quiet calls you."

That quiet called me Wednesday afternoon as Cindy read "You have to go on." It called to me firmly and gently, and I responded with silent tears. Words and memory and beauty, in serendipitous communion.

The poesy of life, and of what it is made.

> And when the time comes
> You have to go on

We knew it was gonna be this way when we came.

Good Lord.

■

Sourdoug

In awe of a loaf of bread? Why, yes. And why not?

Some simple pleasures are apparently older and more basic than we think. Or than I think, anyway. Because I'm dense. Like sourdough.

> The kingdom of heavens is like to sourdough... (Matt. 13:33, Wycliffe Bible, c. 1400)

"Like to sourdough." Yes, it is heavenly.

After a hike at Goat Creek yesterday, Terry L. Pisel and I stopped by the Mazama Store for lunch. Along with the mushroom-and-grain soup that was featured on the menu board, we elected to purchase a loaf of Mazama's oat-sourdough to go along with the meal. I drew the lucky straw to take the remainder home!

> Beware of the sourdough of Pharisees and of Sadducees... (Matt. 16:6, Wycliffe Bible)

A good warning... but you need not beware Mazama's sourdough at all. It's quite good!

I've long been a fan of sourdough bread and was very pleased when, for years running, Jenn would keep starter on hand, direct from San Francisco, and fresh-bake loaves of the stuff. She even wrote about that sourdough, it was so good!

But I've always thought that sourdough bread was sort of "invented" on the American frontier, perhaps during the California Gold Rush, by miners kneading dough with none-too-clean and yeast-infected hands. (I know, right? Yuck!!! But think about it... Things have to be discovered for the first time by accident.)

Boy, was I surprised to read the word *sourdoug* (yes, that's the actual Middle English spelling) several times in yesterday's and today's readings in my Wycliffe New Testament blackletter facsimile. And the word was being used in exactly the sense we use it today: a fermented yeast bread. Hoodathunk?

> Then they understood, that he said not to beware of sourdough of loaves... (Matt. 16:12, Wycliffe Bible)

Some are quicker on the uptake than others, I guess. It was a metaphor, you dummies!

It turns out that, prior to just a couple hundred years ago, if you had raised bread of *any* kind... it was sourdough! That's the only type of yeast bread there was, dating back to thousands of years B.C. So you either had sourdough, or you had flatbread. No other options. Wow.

Which brings me back to that first loaf of sourdough...

■

Jesse Tissell

"We haven't even started yet," declares a downcast sixteen-year-old Jesse, "and the donuts are already gone."

Thus begins the comic "Camping: Unscripted" video on his Crunk Cabin YouTube channel. "They were good until at least August 31st!" his brother-in-law, Josh, also laments. "They had such a life to live."

Crunk Cabin Studios' most popular clip continues with wilderness lessons on "basically starving," with Josh having to gnaw off his own limb ("Poor soul," comments Jesse); diarrhea "and whatnot"; plus "the refrigeration station, the urination station, and the constipation station."

Oh, and there's the fishing. "I don't fish to kill the creatures," clarifies Jesse. "Just to eat 'em."

Jesse is chock full of back-country wisdom, which spills all over the place in his messily witty short films. The first one I ran across was "I Need a Nap or Two," a flannel-shirted Winthrop-hills parody of Ed Sheeran's "Happier."

> My body needs a recharge
> I need a nap or two
> Why does rest feel so far?
> Would shuteye cause me harm?
> My friend sleep and I have grown apart
> Yeah, I need a nap, I do

Now nineteen years old and drawing inspiration from his Methow upbringing and employment at the local Ace Hardware store, Jesse has developed a sharp and entertaining wit. Other recent titles include "Vacation Mode for Hillbillies," "Speeding Ticket Excuses," "I'm Gonna Be a Rapper," and "Dirty Dirty Rednecks" (the latter classified by Crunk Cabin as "Hick Hop").

Yep.

Jesse comes by his comedic chops legitimately. The Tissell family (Mom, Dad, Jesse, and sister, Haleigh) have been producing short films for five years now, and Jesse has been honing his material steadily. The clan's channel now boasts over fifty different entertaining videos! And every once in a while, Jesse will throw in a mention of what's really important to him: not making you laugh, but making sure you know there's a God out there who loves you.

And watching his videos, you'll probably get the impression that Jesse also loves just about everybody. Especially hillbillies.

Not exactly the kind of young man you expect to run into at church.

Though maybe it would be nice if we could.

■

Community

I am often asked how I came to this valley. That has nothing to do with me; it has everything to do with the fact that there are so *many* extraordinary stories of how people came to the Methow. It's just that kind of place. Surprising. Awe-inspiring. People like to hear those stories.

Last night, at a sponsors-only screening of her film *Twisp: The Power of Community*, I had the opportunity to tell Leslee Goodman how I came to the Valley. Given the vision of her film, it was so appropriate.

Goodman, like so many others, also came to the Valley serendipitously and found a certain kind of salvation here—not the eternal kind, the kind that theologians like to argue about, but a very temporal kind, one fueled by nature, by openness to the universe, by love, and by people.

The word "community" is defined as "a feeling of fellowship with others, as a result of sharing common attitudes, interests, and goals." What Goodman discovered here, and what the subjects of her documentary talk about, is life-affirming shared attitudes, interests, and goals: love for the land, for protecting the water and the wildlife, for preserving and honoring ancient things while moving into an uncertain future, for helping each other when need—such as fire or mill closings—arises.

And the inevitable differences?

As obvious as they are on the news and (anti)social media, they are not worth talking about. Life in the Valley, as beautiful as it may be, is not easy, and that's enough; every day has worry enough of its own.

The foodbank and services provided by The Cove are sorely needed; nobody gets rich off farming this land; Diana Hottell, in *The Whole Damn Valley*, wrote extensively about people who came to the Methow and never made enough money to leave; the County has one of the highest incidence rates of youth suicide in the country; and we are far from immune to the meth epidemic.

But Goodman's film is not moony-eyed in telling us our story, telling how this community responds to hardship: not by splintering, but by pulling together. No—it's realistic. As the Valley was counseled in the wake of devastating fires, the future only happens if we rely on each other. If we wait on the outside world to save us, the future will pass us by.

And yet this is not a twisted vision of extrapolated stubborn self-reliance. It's simply a recognition of the way of the world: knowledge that a cord of three strands is not easily broken, that one lies down cold while two or more make for a warm night.

This universe operates on an economy of sharing, of mutual dependence, of reverence for all things; it smiles on us when we cooperate with that economy.

The Power of Community tells so many moving stories, but three stand out. One is the tale of Glenn Schmekel, who moved to Second Mile ranch in 1973, inspired by Jesus' words about doing more than the bare minimum asked—and quickly found out why Poorman Creek is so named. The land may be hard; but Glenn, like so many others, has flourished nonetheless. And as he has found his "place in the natural order of things," as MaMuse sings, and as he has heeded what he hears from the voice of God, the natural order of the Valley has also benefited in the form of The Cove, The Methow Valley Interpretive Center, and reconciliation with the land's native "hosts." Inspiring.

Likewise, it's so moving to hear Hank Konrad talk about the weekend of the Carlton Complex disaster. With hundreds of people fleeing burned homes with nothing in hand and no access to cash, Hank simply went to his safe to find a way to help. "Have you been paid back?" he has been asked. You can tell what the real answer is just by the look in his eyes. Life is so simple, really—not as complicated as we like to make it.

Or how about young Isabel Salas, who tells about the origin of HOPES—Helping Our Peers End Suicide—which was born from the ashes of her own attempts to end her life. She learned that "depression and even suicidal ideation are common, especially in junior and senior high," and determined to make a difference… not just in her life, but in those of others. "We want our peers to know that there is help available, even in such a small community like ours." Wow.

Community. Yeah.

> It starts with a whisper
> Somewhere deep underground
> And it's guaranteed to get louder
> ("The Sound" by Switchfoot)

Thank you, Leslee, and so many who have gone before, for investing in this community, and giving back.

> We, too, are sacred breath made of bone and smoke
> ("Sacred Breath" by MaMuse)

■

Erika Lundahl

I wasn't supposed to be in Winthrop on Saturday.

My plan was to be in Seattle, visiting with family and friends. A last-minute review of pass conditions and five-day weather forecasts persuaded me to change my mind.

Instead, I stayed put and plowed through a long to-do list of work tasks, getting a jump-start on the coming week.

All the while, my radar was revving up. When my plans get chucked out the window, I know something interesting is about to happen.

Mid-afternoon, I wrapped up work and headed out to snowshoe off Balky Hill Road. I had been on the same hillside for a sunset slog through deep powder just a couple days before and wanted to push the trail further toward the summit of the 3000-foot hill named Cap Wright. The going was superb. An inch of fresh powder dusted the track, and in barely more than thirty minutes I had equaled my previous high point. A beaten path helps tremendously; but from there, and for the next 400 to 500 feet of elevation gain, I was once again breaking trail in the wake of the backcountry skier I had followed on Thursday.

My pace slowed noticeably. The blizzard clouds to the west that I had been tracking during the ascent graciously slid to the south without encroaching on the Methow Valley. As I continued up and broke out of the shelter of the sparsely wooded draw and onto open slopes, the sun dramatically shot its rays through breaks in the slate clouds as it drooped slowly toward the peaks of the North Cascades. I pulled on my balaclava and fleece as unobstructed winds swept over the ridgeline from the south, filling the skier's track with spindrift. The crusted snow fractured into plates the weight and thickness of Igloo cooler lids as I plodded on.

Probably less than twenty-five or so vertical feet from the top, I turned back. I was very near my pre-dusk turnaround time, and the final approach to the summit was too exposed and icy for my comfort level and inexperience. As I retraced my way down the summit slope, the beauty of the light and sastrugi overwhelmed me. My upward tracks looked like they dropped off the edge of the world.

Had I really come up that way? Wow.

What was I looking for up here? Had I found it?

I think I had. Unbelievable. Stunning. Wonderstruck by Winter, I thought I'd write.

But the day was not yet done with me.

I showered quickly and checked the Methow Valley activity calendar. Sixknot Organic Hard Cider's Taphouse in Winthrop was hosting musician Erika Lundahl, and a bite to eat from the Sixknot menu sounded awfully appealing.

On the way to Winthrop, I stopped by a friend's house to answer questions about the book *Two Roads Through Narnia*, which I had cowritten long ago. The query was surprising, as

I have not had the occasion to talk about that book in a long, long time. Narnia and snow... a winter without end. Very Methow.

When I arrived at Sixknot and approached the bar to place my order, Erika was on a break between sets and was getting a glass of cider from John, Sixknot's owner. When she and Doug Indrick began their next set, they opened with a cover of Phil Ochs' "When I'm Gone."

> There's no place in this world I'll belong when I'm gone
> And I won't know the right from the wrong when I'm gone
> And you won't find me singin' on this song when I'm gone
> So I guess I'll have to do it while I'm here

The forty-minute set was arresting. Erika's and Doug's music features a mix of original songs and covers, plus a repertoire of musical settings to the words of Edna St. Vincent Millay.

Doug's percussion and backing vocals are spare and not the least bit showy, and even the duo's use of his virtuosic whistling is restrained.

Erika's miked voice cannot mask a power which could easily fill a room unamplified, and she employs a distinctive tapping style on guitar "to create an enveloping, atmospheric musical space," as her website accurately describes. Her songs are filled with a patient passion for humanity and harmony, "the story of who you are now," as she sings in "Abalone Shell."

The duo reflects the wisdom of recovering Pharisees who might have hung out with Jesus back in the day, knowing that, despite all attempts to tighten God's circle like a noose, "communion's open for one and all."

I may have stopped short of the summit earlier that evening; but the real high point of the day—and the set—came when Erika introduced a cover of Coven's "One Tin Soldier." A hush literally came over the room, and you could have heard a feather drop.

> Listen people to a story
> That was written long ago,
> 'bout a kingdom on a mountain
> And the valley folks below.

Every soul in Sixknot, Valley folk all, communed reverently for those four minutes as Erika and Doug poured themselves into a magic moment that they, too, recognized as something divinely appointed. And we all drank deeply of the message beneath the mountain's stone.

The evening concluded, appropriately enough, with a cover of MaMuse.

> We shall be known by the company we keep
> By the ones who circle round to tend these fires
> We shall be known by the ones who sow and reap
> The seeds of change, alive from deep within the earth
>
> It is time now, it is time now that we thrive
> It is time we lead ourselves into the well
> It is time now, and what a time to be alive
>
> In this Great Turning we shall learn to lead in love
> In this Great Turning we shall learn to lead in love

I was not supposed to be in Winthrop Saturday night—but it was nonetheless exactly where I was meant to be.

We indeed shall be known by the ones who sow and reap the seeds of change. What a time to be alive!

■

Appointments

In a Winthrop eatery the other night, I stepped into what's often described as a "divine appointment."

As I sat down to listen to a trio playing covers of 1980s standards, I found an open barstool alongside a man about my age. We engaged in easy conversation between songs, flipping through Trivial Pursuit cards from time to time.

Not long after, the band played a gentle version of an Elvis Costello recording from *Armed Forces*.

> Is all hope lost?
> Is there only pain and hatred, and misery?
> And each time I feel like this inside
> There's one thing I wanna know:
> What's so funny 'bout peace love and understanding?
> Oh, what's so funny 'bout peace love and understanding?

I remarked how surprising it was to hear someone cover that tune in a Winthrop juke joint. My new friend mentioned that his music system at home has a strange tendency to play a lot of Elvis Costello, whom he dislikes; but he knew "Peace, Love and Understanding" and liked it.

"You know," I said, by way of explaining perhaps why he liked this one Costello recording, "the song was actually written by Nick Lowe."

More trivia.

Completely devoid of Costello's typical verbal gymnastics and eschewing Lowe's own trademark smart-ass wit, this early work prefigured the straightforward humanity that would characterize the latter part of Lowe's career. His story is certainly interesting enough, as is Costello's. But more interesting stories than theirs—tales of trial, and tales of survival—were told that night in Winthrop.

You know an extraordinary conversation is taking place when the other party says, "I don't know why I'm opening up to you like I am right now." And you know that the answer is, "Because this conversation needed to happen. I'm not sure why, particularly, but I know it needed to happen."

Perhaps *Rolling Stone*'s words about Nick Lowe's life shine a little light: "It's funny how you can try to plot the phases of your career, or your life, really, and sometimes you end up following the plan as if it's been laid out for you on a map… but always, inevitably, you'll wind up landing in unexpected places."

Like a Winthrop eatery, where the reasons for being there—food, beverage, and music—fade completely into the background while something extraordinary happens instead.

■

Norman Baker

> I wore the wrong pants today
> for getting the job done

So sings Norman Baker in "Bright Gray."

I know the feeling. The last few days have felt like that, with work not exactly going badly—but specific tasks taking way longer than I'd have preferred.

When I finally wound up with a free evening, I debated whether I wanted to go out and catch some music up the Valley, or just stay home and chill. I figured I'd see exactly who Norman Baker was before making a decision about ribs and music at The Methow Valley Ciderhouse.

I visited Baker's webpage and saw that the first track on his latest CD is "Henry Poole." Well, if that ain't a danged omen, I don't know what is. I have written extensively about the film *Henry Poole is Here*, and on multiple occasions. Decision made.

> The past, it is history
> The future is a mystery
> The present is a gift
> Sitting right next to me

Oh, yeah. Like walking into the Ciderhouse and being warmly greeted by Thome George. That man is like a walking good luck charm, because He Requires Art. 'Deed he do. (Though,

I must say, tonight he seemed to require cider and Gonzaga more than music… but hey! cider-making is an art, too, as is a beautiful jumper from three-point range to seal the deal.)

> Saturday night Satan, Sunday saint…
> Come Monday morning it's back to a life of sin

Baker did his sound check with those lines, then came full circle by closing his first set with that tune.

He's kind of a cross between Neil Young—who was himself a little off center, back in his heydey—and They Might be Giants, with every song gifting little lyric surprises. Like the literary version of a kid at the circus, I was audibly hooting at the tastiness of Baker's verbal dexterity. I did wear the wrong pants today for getting the job done; but Norman Baker's music was just the thing I needed to correct that mis-appareling and to conclude a thoroughly righteous Saturday.

I trust that bodes well for Monday, what with the omens and all.

> Every hill faces the right direction,
> but my sole's worn all the way through
> Saints we all are, in truth,
> and everyone comes walking into our yard.

■

Aging

The universe wants us to be amused, too.

After church this morning, I drove up Gunn Ranch Road outside Twisp at the recommendation of George Hoksbergen. He thought the hillsides there would be a good place to scare up some antler sheds.

Rather spontaneously, I found myself doing the Lewis Butte hike—since I had no idea in advance the trail was there. But I was, and it was, so George Mallory and I apparently agree.

The trail is a five-mile round-trip hike with 1000 feet of elevation gain… all on the outward leg. I'm sure glad I did it at the end of March rather than in the depths of July, as it's all switchbacks on wide-open south-facing slopes. Not a bit of shade anywhere.

In the six-plus months I've been in the Methow, this is the first time I've been on a trail shared with more than a couple of people. The early-birds here were hard-core runners whizzing by me on the trail. One dude ran it twice while I was out there. Another runner I had passed on Rendezvous Road… and even he beat me to the top of Lewis Butte, passing me both on the way up *and* his way back down before I topped out.

Even though I chugged right along and only stopped for a snack because I was hungry and it was 1:00 PM, not because

I was tired, I was definitely feeling old in comparison to these athletic upper-Methow twenty-some-things. Fortunately, on the way down I encountered ordinary families and couples. This made me feel a little less cardiovascularly inferior.

One couple in particular I ended up playing leapfrog with a few times, as I was stopping to shoot photos and they were fond of shortcuts on the switchbacks. The young mother had her toddler in a carrier on her back, and they were walking with two mismatched pugs.

The last time I ran across them, I had my zoom lens attached to my camera body to shoot closeups of butterflies and flowers. As they traversed the slope below me, I heard the mother remark, "Well, when *we're* old and have nothing better to do with our time, we can get a camera with a big old lens and take as long as we want shooting photos!"

I chuckled to myself, understanding that she probably thought 150 yards was far enough away to not be overheard... but she probably hadn't taken the wind into account. "I heard that!" I called down the slope with a laugh.

"I didn't mean it that way!" she hollered back apologetically.

Strange that her voice carried so well up the slope even though her husband's didn't. But apparently her original remark had been in response to her daughter's question about why they weren't stopping to take pictures. "All we have is a little point-and-shoot."

Just before they passed around the ridgeline and out of earshot, her final muttered remark to her husband was, "I guess it probably did sound a little bad, didn't it?"

I just paused and had a good long laugh.

Yes, I suppose it is pretty cool to be older and have all the time in the world to stand around and shoot photos.

I'll take it.

Shannon Huffman Polson

I fully expected to be writing at some point about Methow Valley resident and writer Shannon Huffman Polson, but I did not expect it to be today.

> I hear the voices around me. I am swallowed up in them. I close my eyes and sink into the sound slowly, like a sigh.

I was pleasantly surprised when I first moved to Twisp to find that Shannon was a local. I had been aware of Shannon for some time due to her presence on the faith-market blog conglomerate *Patheos*, which plays host to a number of former colleagues from my journalism days. Shannon was also based in Seattle for a number of years, during which time she rubbed elbows with several of our mutual journalist acquaintances.

Shannon has not only been a prominent blogger and author, she also happens to have been one of the first women to fly the Army's Apache attack helicopters. She's been a mountaineer, a poet, wife, and mother, and is now a public speaker and founder of the Grit Project, which you may have seen featured on *Today*.

In addition to our shared membership in Confluence Poets, Shannon and I have finally had the opportunity to cross paths and chat briefly a few times in recent weeks. After lunching with my brother, Bob, and nephew Robert in Winthrop Sunday afternoon, it occurred to me on my way home that I needed some new reading material. Shannon's books came to mind.

Back I drove to Winthrop and Trail's End Bookstore. I made a beeline for the "Local Authors" table and picked up a couple volumes, including Shannon's *North of Hope*, the autobiographical account of her trip down the Arctic's Hulahula River in search of closure while grieving the grizzly-mauling death of her father and stepmother on the same river a year prior.

I began reading the book Sunday night, then last evening had a message exchange with a good friend about the end of a hopeful relationship. This morning I read words in *North of Hope* that I thought might be of solace.

"Nowhere is it guaranteed," Shannon writes, "that a blessing comes with comfort."

This was wisdom that I thought I should pass along to my friend, completely unaware that within a few minutes those words would also have profound and immediate meaning for me.

It has been a long morning. When I came back to that page a short while ago, Shannon's further metaphor resonated deeply: "I had quit my tent and come here for God; maybe I wasn't prepared for what he would say or how he would say it. Maybe I wasn't prepared for what he would not say."

Wow. Yes. Late last year, I quit my own tent on the Westside and came to Twisp for God… and all along, there has been no way I could have prepared for what he would say or how he would say it.

And today, in particular, I was caught completely flat-footed—in full knowledge of how I have been blessed, yet lacking the specific and selfish comfort I have craved.

What an incredibly timely reminder from Shannon that we often think wrongly about the nature of blessing.

> The search for comfort can be so misleading… and the search for blessing so rewarding, nonetheless. Surely each of us here has a grief for which they sing, whether or not they know it.

∎

Pressure

"WOW," a friend commented privately in response to yesterday's Note about Shannon Huffman Polson.

"Yes," was my response. "It's gonna be one of those days." I must have been psychic.

"I can't recall where," I continued, "but over the last week I've been hearing a lyric over and over, something about 'seeing things as they are' and finding the blessings in them rather than seeing what is not and wishing for that. It's more than the 'glass half-full' idea. More like the crisis of perception that calls the glass half-empty in the first place.

"*A priori* commitments matter most," I concluded, "when they are tested, not while resting in one's easy chair."

The specific *a priori* commitment of which I was thinking when I wrote that was the ideal of selfless love; my musing about it was spurred by a dream I had during the previous night and by running across the David Bowie + Queen hit "Under Pressure" during my morning Facebook crawl.

There are many reasons to be struck by the track, by Queen, by David Bowie, even by Annie Lennox and her performance of the song with Bowie at the Freddie Mercury tribute in 1992.

But for the purposes of today's essay…

I never fail to be waylaid by the depth of emotion which stirs within me when "Under Pressure" surges toward the last stanza, set up by Freddie's question:

> Can't we give ourselves one more chance?
> Why can't we give love that one more chance?
> Why can't we give love…

Bowie replies:

> 'Cause love's such an old fashioned word
> And love dares you to care for
> The people on the edge of the night
> And love dares you to change our way of
> Caring about ourselves

Yes. Love is a dare. As with blessing, as Shannon noted, love is not a comfortable proposition. It comes with a promise of testing.

What will you do when the chips are down? Will you really respond selflessly, with good will, regardless of the personal cost?

I heard "Under Pressure" on the radio again last night after an unbelievable day that became even more surreal and challenging as the evening progressed.

I think I can safely say that testing is easier to endure when you've been properly equipped for the event. And yesterday my unlooked-for equipment included *North of Hope* and "Under Pressure."

So be it.

This is our last dance
This is our last chance
This is ourselves
Under pressure

Theater

Stephen Kish is Technical Director at The Merc Playhouse in Twisp. I'll be working with him on *A Diner on the Way*, which hits the boards in July.

Plain old "Kish" spent several seasons as stage manager at McMurdo Station. In Antarctica.

He first came to Winthrop by walking there. From Mexico.

That's 2600 miles on the Pacific Crest Trail, with his wife.

What a wacky place the Methow is. It figures that I'm in rehearsals again, for the first time in sixteen years. After all, when I moved to Twisp I told everyone who would listen, "No, I'm done with theater. I have no desire to act again, or direct." And I was deadly serious.

Doing a show will suck up three months of your life in a heartbeat. I guess the universe figures I have months to spare.

Out of the blue a month or so ago, Joel Douglas Moreland texted me. "Hey, if you have an open role in a show you're doing let me know. I'd love to do some acting again!" I looked at my phone like it was an alien.

"Now where in the hell did Douglas get the idea that I'm doing theater?" thought I. "I haven't said anything about that to anyone on the Westside. And all I've said over here is 'No way!'" I dismissed it as an aberration.

The following Sunday I ran into Joel Hylback at church. I'd only met him once before, via our mutual friend Molly H. Lachapelle. We started talking, and somehow, within just a couple of minutes, the conversation turned to theater. "So how do you see your writing fitting into the local theater scene?" asked Joel.

I remember blinking a couple of times, before I stammered something like, "Well, I don't really have any plans to do that. But it's funny you should ask…" I had actually handed off a copy of my three-act *Measure for Measure* to Merc board member Jane Hill a couple weeks earlier because Merc founder Carolanne Steinebach had asked if I had any scripts the theater might produce.

When I got home from church, I had a message from Jane. "Greg, I know you're not wanting to do any acting, but we've got an open role in the upcoming show, and everyone thinks you'd be perfect for it. It's an offstage voice."

It's flattering to know that I'd be perfect offstage… but I took the hint.

And I took the part, continuing my long history of never getting parts I audition for but getting invited to play all kinds of roles. I have been cast as Burt in *A Diner on the Way*… a script which twice features lines from *Measure for Measure*. Uh-huh.

I've been in rehearsals for two weeks now, and I'm remembering what I loved about theater in the first place. When you're in rehearsals and when you're on stage, you get a chance to focus in ways that ordinary life doesn't let you—

unless you get out on the trail or live in an isolated place like McMurdo Station.

Rehearsal is a kind of meditation and mindfulness, a concentrated dose of learning about yourself and about others.

Director Mark Easton gave me the night off rehearsal Thursday, which gave me the chance to catch another bit of theater—Cindy Williams Gutiérrez' *In the Name of Forgotten Women*, "a choreopoem combining poetry with music and dance," the poetry have been taken from the text of her latest volume, *Inlay with Nacre*.

Cindy is one of the Confluence Poets, of which I am also a member, and I was so glad to be able to support her by being on hand for the sold-out event, produced at Wellspring by Tracy Sprauer.

One sequence was particularly moving—"Mothers Against the Dirty War," a screed about the 30,000 "disappeared" of Argentina's Operation Condor in the late 1970s and early 1980s. The sequence was taken from Cindy's "An Embarrassment of Euphemisms," with the cast emphatically pronouncing "five words into a knot of truth": *desaparecido, torturado, asesinado, nunca olvidado*. Disappeared. Tortured. Assassinated. Never forgotten.

During a Q&A following the show, the comfort of the performance space was debated a bit. "Theater and poetry are provocation," I offered. "One of the problems of art is that as it gets 'bigger' it gets more comfortable. One of the great things about the Methow is that even superb art stays small here. It's intimate. And if the performance spaces aren't necessarily ideal, that's actually for the better. This experience isn't supposed to be comfortable."

My sister, Elane, is in town this weekend. She met Stephen last night at The Old Schoolhouse Brewery in Winthrop where we were enjoying fish and chips while Stephen was producing the evening's musical entertainment—Hillfolk Noir, a folk combo out of Idaho featuring upright bass, harmonica, washboard, and saw. Yep.

Tonight, Elane and I are seeing the local high school's production of *Chicago* at The Merc.

Yeah. I think Theater and I have a thing goin'.

Casting

At sixteen years old, I was cast as Mr. Darling in our high school production of *Peter Pan*.

I had been on a three-year theater hiatus since ninth grade—but after I dropped band, my senior year schedule allowed time to get back on the boards.

In addition to my performance as the insufferable Mr. Darling, I took the role of Smee, although classic casting for this show usually doubles Mr. Darling up with Hook; but that lead role went to Greg Fisher, given his strong experience with musicals.

As much theater as I have done, this remains the only show in which I was actually awarded a role following auditions. Every other time I have auditioned, I have been passed over.

Instead, I have consistently made a theater "career" out of being recruited to fill roles that directors have not been able to cast for one reason or another.

My first adult experience was Sherlock Holmes in *The Hound of the Baskervilles* at Redwood Theater (then in Bothell). I had spied the audition notice in a "movie news" rag at the Cinerama in 1988 while waiting for *The Last Temptation of Christ* to roll. When I later followed up by phone with director (and Redwood founder) Wendy Los, I discovered that I would be in Kansas City on business during auditions.

Wendy nonetheless suggested that I circle back upon my return, in case auditions did not pan out. They did not.

Wendy invited me to her condo to read with her—and, lo! and behold, I found myself taking on Holmes at the raw age of 26. The show broke attendance records with standing-room-only crowds, standing ovations, and rave reviews. I honestly think that Steve Brozene's Watson was the best part of the show—but the entire cast did have rare chemistry, the result of Wendy's all-around brilliant casting.

I would go on to work with all of those artists again multiple times, but none so often as Melanie Calderwood. It was she who invited me to take another pivotal lead shortly thereafter, as Simon Peter in *This Rock*, an apocryphal examination of the saint-to-be's suicidal state in the hours between the Crucifixion and Resurrection.

The show was being produced for Good Friday at Melanie's church, and by that time I had learned to trust her instincts implicitly. She didn't tell me, however, one bit about the role or the play before I showed up for the table read... which was quite an eye-opener. I had my own issues with guilt, depression, and suicidal ideation at the time, and the script threatened to break open spiritual and emotional floodgates.

In spite of my Method-ish approach to getting inside Peter's head, I kept the role at arm's length through rehearsals, unable to wholly commit to *being* Peter. It scared me.

It all flowed out during the performance, however. Backstage afterward, I could not stop sobbing. Fellow actors consoled me for fifteen or twenty minutes.

The emotion of that single performance sticks with me to this day and drove most of what I did in theater for the next ten years.

These are the kinds of things that happen when you don't audition.

Another example a couple years later was *Cat's Cradle*, a mystery by Leslie Sands. I was producing the show, as well as doing set and lighting design. I assisted director Jim Davis during auditions, and at the end of three long-slog nights he took a serious look at me and said, "Why don't you read?"

For some reason, I have an impossible time saying "No" in such circumstances. I read, and the rest was history. CID inspector John Frost became one of the darkest characters I have played.

I noted last week that the same type of thing has pretty much happened again here in Twisp with The Merc Playhouse. I am not sure if it is my reputation or my gullibility that precedes me…

…because I found myself at rehearsal Monday night all prepped to be off-book for my off-stage voice role as Burt in *A Diner on the Way* and found director Mark Easton looking me directly in the eye as he announced that one of our follow cast members had withdrawn from the play.

We found ourselves in need of an older gentleman onstage, and in a fairly urgent way. "Well, who's going to play Wally?" someone asked.

"We have our Wally!" Mark proudly announced, without bothering to ask me first. And I had been early to rehearsal!

How could I say no? I know—by using my lips and voice.

But I like to be flattered by the impression that directors have confidence in me... even if the primary emotion which leads them to call on my services is desperation rather than confidence. Ha!

After rehearsal, Mark and his wife, LaShelle, confessed that they'd debated whether to consult with me first or just spring it on me.

I didn't ask for an explanation. I just chose to be entertained.

How could I not be? I am a slave to surprise.

■

Ian Maclaren

At the last meeting of Confluence Poets, Christine Kendall brought me a gift—a vintage edition of Ian Maclaren's *Beside the Bonnie Brier Bush*. She had found it while browsing in a used book store and thought of me.

With Cindy Williams Gutiérrez and another friend, we had attended the Burns Supper in Mazama in January, so Christine is well acquainted with my fondness for all things Scottish.

> Conversation with us was a leisurely game, with slow movements and many pauses, and it was our custom to handle all the pawns before we brought the queen into action.

Maclaren is a new author to me—but he is immensely quotable, and he writes in *Brier Bush* of subjects dear to my heart: small-town rural life; Perthshire, Tayside, and the Cairngorms; country lanes and quiet sunsets; humility and peacefulness; stoicism in the face of suffering; respect and admiration for women; genuine brotherhood; and faith.

> I suppose that there is nothing in a human life so precious to God, neither clever words nor famous deeds, as the sacrifices of love.

That Maclaren should appeal to me is not surprising. He was himself a pastor, and his real name was John Watson.

(Remember: I played Sherlock Holmes!)

He began his public career roughly at the same time as Booth Tarkington and Francis Thompson, both favorite writers of mine. He was also a contemporary of George MacDonald, whose work was influential on J.R.R. Tolkien and C.S. Lewis. I rather imagine they read Maclaren as well, given his immense popularity and the subject matter of his work.

> Drumtochty gave itself to a "beerial" with chastened satisfaction, partly because it lay near to the sorrow of things, and partly because there was nothing of speculation in it.

Maclaren writes of the apparently fictional village of Drumtochty, Perthshire, after the same fashion that Faulkner writes of Yoknapatawpha County, Sherwood Anderson writes of Winesburg, or Tarkington writes of Plattville. While the locales may be fictional in many or all respects, an attentive reader can tell that all the details are firmly rooted in true experience. Young writers are often counseled to "write what you know," and for good reason. Truth may be stranger than fiction, but fiction that is disconnected from life rings hollow.

> Texts I can never remember, nor, for that matter, the words of sermons; but the subject was Jesus Christ, and before he had spoken five minutes, I was convinced, who am outside dogma and churches, that Christ was present.

In researching Maclaren/Watson, I am not surprised to find that I am familiar with his work after all. One does not sell millions of books without something of one's impact left for generations that follow.

If you pay attention to social media memes at all, you will at least be familiar with this closing quote, which originates with Maclaren:

> Be kind, for everyone you meet is fighting a hard battle.

So very true, and so very applicable—as I was reminded this weekend while visiting with a friend who is at her mother's side through the long decline of hospice care.

Thank you, Christine, for this very timely gift.

Wonderstruck!

Jennifer Epps

Jennifer Epps is one-half the performing duo of Notable Exceptions.

I met Jennifer for the first time just over a week ago… but I have labored long over writing this Wonderstruck note because there were so many remarkable things about that meeting.

> Once I rode the foothills
> And I swung a long reata
> I worked the hide and tallow trade
> in the land I loved
> I rode in wooden stirrups
> And the dust raised by my ponies
> Was smoke, from my altar offered up to the God above

Notable Exceptions was performing at a house concert at the home of Teri Pieper and Ken Bevis… so I considered writing "Wonderstruck by House Concerts," because the intimacy of such a setting is a wonderful thing for both performer and audience member. Artists can be confident that patrons are present to actually listen to the music, rather than shout over drinks at a crowded bar while they make plans for what they'll do after the music is done… and listeners have the unusual opportunity, if they avail themselves, to talk at length with musicians before and after sets.

I also might have written "Wonderstruck by Teri Pieper," given the brilliance of her own artistic work behind the lens of a camera. (I still may.)

Or "Wonderstruck by Ken Bevis," because, well, who isn't? On this particular night, Ken did a brilliant job of promoting the work of other artists. He is a tireless promoter of the arts, and advocate for patronage of artists. Love it!

I might also have written "Wonderstruck by Dave Stamey," the author of the lyrics I excerpt in this essay.

I learned about Stamey that night because Notable Exceptions included Stamey's "The Vaquero Song" as the third number of their opening set. Jennifer and her partner, Judy Coder, brought the room's collective heart to a standstill with their moving, heartfelt cover of the "modern classic," and I made a mental note to ask one of them about the song later, as I wasn't sure who wrote it or what the title was.

What I did know was that Jennifer owned that song, as surely as if she were its protagonist.

"Wonderstruck by the Methow Valley" also might have done, as the dusky sunset view from Ken and Teri's porch railing offered a 270-degree view from the Chewuch confluence down past the Twisp confluence. I met Jennifer there by the railing between sets, and she told me about the song, and about Juan Medina, Stamey's fictional and titular vaquero.

> Beyond the sagging ruins of these adobe walls
> You may see me in the dust,
> That shimmers in the half light
> Or hear me in the whisper, of the grass so green and tall

Thinking about this song, and writing about it, brings me to tears once more. I am so grateful to have heard it performed by Notable Exceptions, at a house concert, in the company of good friends like Ken and Teri. I am thankful for the opportunity to talk with Jennifer and learn more about Stamey and his music.

But I did settle on "Wonderstruck by Jennifer Epps." Not just because of her skill with the guitar, snoot flute, yodeling, Indian flute, recorder, and "other stuff," and not just because of her sweet, sweet harmonization. Or because of the well-honed cowgirl stage persona that is part of Notable Exceptions.

I am wonderstruck by Jennifer Epps because of her humanity. Because, as you stand in the golden hour light by an epic valley view, she looks you in the eye and holds it. Because she is a human being.

Because, for that night at least, and today, she reminds me that after all we go through, we are, like that vaquero, still here. And that counts for a lot.

> Oh, I mingle with each grain of sand
> in the land that is my birthright
> I am still here, todavía estoy aquí
> I am still here, todavía estoy aquí

■

A Coen Dream

I spent (almost) the entire night in a Coen brothers film.

The dream movie was a farcical engineering workplace scenario in which the company had been acquired in a hostile takeover... which proved highly lucrative for all the employees. All, that is, except me.

While top Dilbert-like management all got sacked immediately, the "get-even" plot of the venture capital team involved a pay-for-play severance package. If that doesn't make any sense, remember that this was a Coen Bros. film.

So this was the deal. Every bit of engineering that had been done for the original owners had to be re-written from the ground up, due to the original owners' refusal to sell their intellectual property—tedious work enough, but the carrot was this: You'd get paid four times your normal salary for the work, for however long it took.

Everybody was thrilled, including me, since we were all already getting paid top-tier rates. (How this was to be an advantage to the VC folks... well, welcome to Coen land.)

But I go back to my workspace only to remember... I was a Dilbert in a Dilbert company and had somehow managed to never actually write a deliverable line of code in my entire time of employment. So now I was repeating my make-work scenario to earn my keep... knowing I would pe paid zippo.

Farce upon farce. Truly worthy of a *Hudsucker*-like Coen Bros. film. This dream literally went on almost all night. Up until 4:37. That's when I woke up, looked at the clock, and then promptly went back to sleep.

The next half hour was absorbed in the making of a self-referential meta film (yeah, you industry types know what that means) in which I was employed by a Pixar-like company making a feature film about a UPS-like shipping company. The film was called *Boxed*. Get it? Like *Cars*.

In the second feature of the night's program, my name is Ted, and I am a John Cusack-like story consultant… overseeing the most abysmally stupid storyline ever conceived. Not only are the stars of the live-action story actual shipping containers (voiced by the people who move them, because live-action boxes can't actually move themselves), but all of the film company executives have co-starring roles as… the shipping company executives (in yet another stunning cost-savings move).

The culminating "action" (ha!) sequence of the film involves the "youngest" box of the crew assisting in a "dangerous" mechanical repair of a state-of-the-art shipping van (yes! black is the new Brown!) and a "false hazard" (oh, no! the box might get stuck in the tire well behind the front fender!) as rising tension.

This is an exaggerated satirical take on the standard Pixar plotline, in case you hadn't noticed.

In a control-room setting not unlike the Def Con war room of *War Games*, the shipco execs (including me, Ted), look on in the grip of "terror" as little Boxie is, uh, miraculously freed from his little ol' jam. As he is released from the grip of death, he falls over onto the floor in exhaustion.

This stunner is captured on the big screen in the control room, in a faux reality TV-like setting. A crisply labeled box which might conceivably contain a small fire extinguisher flops over onto a concrete floor. And the camera holds that "dramatic" shot as Boxie sighs. Oh, Lord.

Problem is, I, Ted, have my back to the camera, looking incredulously at the faces of my co-execs with mouth hanging open and eyebrows arched while all my colleagues are hamming up their relief… in the face of an absurd third act of their own design. Again, picture a Cusack-like story consultant, thinking, "You've got to be joking."

The film closes with the Nurse Ratched-like senior executive announcing via intercom that disaster has been averted and that shipping can now resume… and pointedly commenting, "Edward Batchelor, please return your attention to the front of the control room."

Wow. Yes, I (Ted) get reprimanded by Nurse Ratched in the way that a mother might do. "Edward Batchelor, please return your attention to the front of the control room."

Where does this stuff come from?

■

Cristofori's Dream

What a day.

I stood in the Great Room at Twisp Terrace Lodge, alone, a baby grand piano in the corner. Dramatic evening light spilled through gaps in clouds racing across McClure Mountain and the hills up Twisp River. Tears welled in my eyes.

Because David Lanz's "Cristofori's Dream" was playing over the Lodge's sound system.

Intending to settle in and read a bit in mountaineer Don Whillans' autobiography while I awaited the arrival of several friends, I had no sooner exchanged a few words with the bartender when the "Dream" began… and it was as if I were, in fact, in the midst of a most wonderful dream.

My day had begun with the luxury of sleeping in without an alarm to rouse me. Coming off several weeks of round-the-clock deadlines the extra sleep was a decided luxury. After a quick wrap-up of morning's work and a tasty treat of fresh scones and all-natural local raspberry jam, I wrote "Erratic," a wonderful little thought-poem which I dedicated to its inspiration, Jon Hawley.

Some weeding in my drive, a quick shower, and a call with a new business partner—and then I loaded up some gear and a Beecher's cheese and ham sandwich to lunch along the banks of the Methow south of town.

After picking up a calzone and no-wheat peanut butter and chocolate chip cookie at Cinnamon Twisp Bakery for my dinner at rehearsal, I drove a bit down Twisp-Carlton Road to read in the shade of riverbank saskatoon and pine as the clouds scudded by to the north.

Following stops for errands at Confluence Gallery in Twisp and The Iron Horse in Winthrop, I was off to a meeting of Confluence Poets at Rocking Horse Bakery. The work was brisk and engaging, and the opportunity to exchange hugs with friends sweet. On the way home, I dropped Ryan Brennan at the wonderful little home he shares with his sister on a west-facing bluff above Twisp River on 2nd Avenue.

At home, I wrapped up the last details of my day's work and then drove up to Twisp Terrace. Along the way, I stopped by Jon and Charlene's place to drop off a copy of "Erratic." Jon told me I had "made his day."

Oh, he had no idea. The day had been wonderful for me already, and I knew the peacefulness of the pub would crown things nicely.

I was not expecting "Cristofori's Dream," however. How could I? How could anybody?

If there is any piece of music that reminds me of Jenn, it is this. She performed it as part of the piano recital which I produced for her at Normandy ArtsFest in 1996, and her recording of "Cristofori's Dream" streams from my MP3-player from time to time. The song is rhythmic and pensive, containing melodies and harmonies both somber and hopeful.

Lanz spoke to Jenn's soul in this piece, and when Jenn wrote of the "88 keys to her heart," this music expressed that feeling better than any other.

Eric Blank approached me as tears welled in my eyes. I explained the source of my emotion.

"I didn't know that was the name of this song," he replied. "I used to listen to my sister practice this at the piano all the time."

As Eric returned to his rounds, I returned my gaze to the view out the Great Room's picture window, soaking in the spirit of the scene and the moment.

The day only got better. After a bit of reading, a flood of good friends arrived for dinner—Candy and George, Nancy and Jim, Kristi and Don, Bonnie and Don. A quick pint of cider for me, though, and I was off to another rehearsal of *A Diner on the Way* at The Merc Playhouse—our first really complete off-book run-through of the whole show.

The calzone and cookie were a fine choice for my on-stage meal!

As I walked out onto Glover Street after rehearsal, I was blown away. Dark storm clouds had flooded up the Methow from the south during rehearsal—but as the sun was setting behind the North Cascades, it sent shafts of Golden Hour light bathing Balky Hill, Cap Wright, and Mill Hill in the richest hues imaginable.

Never before have the hills east of Twisp looked so gorgeous.

Cristofori's dream... is it mine? So rich is the music of life. How blessed I am.

After gassing up at Hank's, I spied one of my favorite people in the world dashing into the parking lot to grab groceries before the market's closing. We parked facing each other and got out to share an embrace and a quick chat. The perfect ending to a perfect day.

This afternoon, raindrops pelt against my window as I write. Lighting flashes from time to time and thunder rumbles as the storm clouds continue to stream over McClure Mountain up the Methow from the south. A flash flood alert has just been transmitted to cell phones in the Valley.

Magic. And danger. The right hand, and the left. They are both there in "Cristofori's Dream."

They are both there in my dream, too. Where is there ever magic without danger? Cristofori must have created the piano for such days as this.

■

Westendorf

One late winter evening, I wandered into Sixknot Taphouse and discovered that the Westendorf Trio was playing.

I ordered a pint and a cidered bratwurst and settled in to enjoy the jazz of Lynette Westendorf on piano, Howie Johnson on bass, and Kirk Schumacher on drums. About eight other people were there with me.

To call the setting "intimate" would be a gross understatement as chit-chat between the musicians and the patrons peppered the two sets I caught.

Watching Lynette work the keyboard fascinated me, and I'm terribly surprised to find that I have not yet written about that evening. I believe I expected a poem to flow out of the experience, something centered on the "sustainability" of music—under the influence of the way that Lynette works the pedal (and her feet in general) as she plays. Her musical intensity couples with her lightness of being and spirit (and the slightness of her build!) in a fashion that reminds me greatly of Jenn and how much I enjoyed watching her play.

Liz Adams Johnson's guy, Howie, calls himself an "amateur" on the bass, which simply means he didn't start seriously playing until coming to the Methow—but anybody who's caught the trio (and happily paid for the privilege) knows that adjective to be humbly self-misapplied.

When Kirk was absent from the lineup the next time I caught the Trio, I surely missed him. This is a tight combo, and their repertoire is deep and rich. I can't really say that I know a damn thing about jazz, having only scant experience with the genre while playing alto sax in junior high and high school jazz bands; but I do know musical excellence of all stripes when I encounter it, and I treasure the opportunity to see musicians work up close during live performance—something of a specialty of the Methow.

Lynette, by contrast, has made music her life. Hailing from a tiny Idaho town, as I understand it, her talent took her to the Big City, formal training, and long experience as a professional musician. A few months ago, when I started asking around about who might be able to advise me about the specifics of orchestral instrumentation, several people immediately suggested that Lynette's knowledge would run the deepest. At the closing concert of the most recent Methow Valley Chamber Music Festival at Liz and Howie's Signal Hill Ranch, Lynette read the Weston Gaylord text of the festival's "Prologue" to open the program while the musicians played a brand new Westendorf composition for "Prologue" behind her. Locally, she is ubiquitous.

She won a Northwest Emmy award for her scoring of *False Promises: The Lost Lands of the Wenatchi*, and her compositions have been performed worldwide. She was a founding member of Seattle's Composers and Improvisers Workshop.

Most recently, I picked up a couple of her CDs at the Confluence Gallery's "Alley Sale." The title track of *Mystery in a Gray Room* (2007) opens and closes with variations on the tune of "Fairest Lord Jesus."

> Fair is the sunshine, fairer still the moonlight
> And all the twinkling starry host

"Stars," she told *Methow Grist*'s Solveig Torvik some years ago, were the reason she and her husband, E. Richard Hart, came to the Methow. "We needed to be in a rural environment," she expanded. *Mystery in a Gray Room* was recorded while Lynette was in residence in the Methow, so I suspect she found what she and Richard were looking for.

> Fair are the meadows, fairer still the woodlands
> Robed in the blooming garb of spring
> Jesus is fairer, Jesus is purer
> Who makes the woeful heart to sing

I'll be catching The Westendorf Trio again soon. If your heart is woeful, you might also consider dropping in to find some help in making it sing.

Geez. What a treat. Wonderstruck.

∎

Authenticity

I stopped by Confluence Gallery yesterday afternoon on my way to a meeting in Winthrop.

I was there to look at jewelry, as I wanted to pick up a ring for my character, Wally, to wear in The Merc Playhouse's production of *A Diner on the Way*. (Before last night, I'd been using Tony Love's personal ring, but I forgot to return it to him Saturday night; I'd hate to lose somebody else's personal property!)

While I was browsing around, Rose Weagant asked how I was feeling about the upcoming performance after three nights off. Her daughter Magnolia Brown appears in the show with me as Elly Hubbard, so the question was pretty natural. I told her I was looking forward to it, which I was, of course.

"Are you nervous?" Rose asked.

"No, not at all," I replied. "I used to get terribly anxious about going on stage, but I don't anymore."

"I find that little bit of nervous energy to be pretty useful," Rose observed.

"True enough," I agreed. "And I used to really feed off of that," I continued.

"But these days I tend to go more on a feeling of quiet confidence."

I would prefer to report that "quiet confidence" is the byproduct of some zen-like project that started at some specific point in my life and reached culmination after years of diligent work. But that's simply not the case.

I could—and have, in recent weeks, while talking to people about how different doing theater is now after twenty years of my life have passed—mention a good many changes that have transpired during those years. But they are all tied up in one simple fact: The fifteen years of my late wife's catastrophic illness, which took us out of theater (and a great many other things), were a mighty crucible.

The "refiner's fire" is both a potent literal force and a powerful (and terrifying) literary and scriptural metaphor. Quite honestly, being thrust white-hot into the forge is something that very few people actively search out; picture, if you will, the Ring of Power melting in the fires of Orodruin at the end of *The Return of the King*. Yep. Inspiring, isn't it?

Sure, we all have our weak points, imperfections, and even "impurities." But do you really want all those burned away? Doesn't it sound a lot more appealing to just work on them gradually and piecemeal with the aid of self-help books, weekly Bible studies, gentle meditation, or Oprah? Getting thrown into the deep end is an awfully dangerous way to learn to swim, to deliberately mix metaphors.

I thought about this effect in my own life as I drove from Twisp to Winthrop—and it struck me that what really got burned away through the final years of Jenn's life, particularly during the eighteen months of near-daily grand mal seizures that Jenn endured, was pretense.

If there is anything missing in foxholes, it's fakery.

Until very recent years, I have spent most of my life feeling like a fraud, terrified that I might be exposed as a hack, a pretender, a wanna-be—immensely unqualified to be a project manager, a theater director, a pastor, a teacher, a film critic, a lecturer, an actor—a husband.

Underlying all of that, the great question: Who am I, really?

When Jenn passed away the day before Thanksgiving at the end of 2017, this is literally the only answer I was left with for that question: a caregiver; a truly loving husband; the hand of God, in a very small but decidedly meaningful way. Aside from that, I honestly couldn't have told you who I was or what I enjoyed.

But coming out of the crucible, that little bit was enough—because it was *real*. The rest had indeed burned away.

From there, and through the help of very good friends and a merciful Father, I have rediscovered who I really am and what really matters to me.

Further, I have been mightily blessed to have done that here, in the Methow—a home which I discovered one year ago today.

So now, when I go on stage or read poetry or sit in on board meetings, I'm not afraid of being exposed. Because *I already am*.

I am who I am. And that is enough… but only because who I am today is simply a stopping point on my way to becoming someone else!

I can't wait to see who that's going to be… because my quiet confidence is not in self; it's in a universe that never fails to surprise me.

∎

Cello... and Poetry

Confluence Poets meet twice a month, once in Twisp and once in Winthrop.

We conduct a little business, and then someone brings a "prompt" for some on-the-spot writing, which we share with one another. Following that, we each read a prepared poem-in-progress that we bring for group critique.

After yesterday's meeting at Rocking Horse Bakery, Subhaga Crystal Bacon and I adjourned to Sixknot Taphouse for a pint, a snack, and some engaging conversation. Afterward, we rendezvoused with Christine Kendall at Shafer Museum for a cello concert produced in association with the Methow Valley Chamber Music Festival.

Artistic Director Kevin Krentz and his brand-new wife, Haeyoon Shin, are instructors at Seattle Cello Academy, and they brought their students to the Methow for a summer cello camp and four nights of performances at different venues. Last night's at the Shafer was the first.

Christine, Subhaga, and I sat under the shady eaves of "Guy Waring's Castle" in perfect summer temperatures for the hour-long performance.

For the third piece, a teenaged cellist performed Giovanni Sollima's "Lamentatio," which, as the title suggests, is a mournful piece—for both solo cello and solo voice. There are no lyrics; but with a lamentation, who needs words? Yet the experience of that performance demands words.

A day steeped in poetry and conversation, the peacefulness of the Shafer lawn, the shade of Waring's Castle, the company of good friends, the artistry of Krentz, Shin, and their students—the moan of the bow on the strings alternating with plucking, strumming, and voice… remarkable.

> The boy cellist bows his neck
> over the neck of his cello, his cut-velvet
> hair catching July light
> as he plays and sings

Subhaga wrote those words upon returning home in "Lamentation for Cello Choir."

> Such a paradox, this combination
> of youth and grief; it plucks at my heart
> like pizzicato, pulling out
> all the love and loss of sixty years.

Yes—a wracking of loss, and love. "The cello is a serious business," she concludes,

> an ancient ritual, where sound
> speaks in the words we've lost,
> all the words we've not yet found.

After the performance, I leaned in to Subhaga and whispered, "If I die before you do, you can read a poem at my memorial after a performance of 'Lamentatio.'"

It was that good. That worth remembering.

Remarkable.

Just another day in the Methow.

∎

Mountainfilm

A warm summer night at an outdoor theater in the North Cascades watching a feature film about the Grand Canyon, along with a hundred or so other outdoor enthusiasts, cuddling under a blanket with a woman who loves me.

Wow. I think I'll just stop right there.

Okay, maybe not. Mountainfilm presents an annual roadshow featuring mostly short films about the "indomitable spirit" of outdoor recreation, curated from their annual festival in Telluride. One of their first stops is a weekend-long event at Mazama Ranch, including three nights of outdoor screenings plus two afternoon events in the Ranch's barn. Evening events include freshly prepared foods and Saturday night live music.

Last night's program featured *National Geographic* photographer Pete McBride's feature-length film *Into the Canyon*, which documents his 2016 traverse of the Grand Canyon rim with frequent journalist companion Keven Fedarko.

I know, right? *Into the Canyon* outdoors, under Methow stars.

I of course have a natural affinity for the subject matter. I'd already read the article in *National Geographic*, so I knew what to expect from the rather insane project McBride and Fedarko undertook as relative Canyon neophytes.

Established trails at the Canyon mostly run from rim to floor and back again—not along the rim itself. While the river runs about 250 miles through the National Park, an end-to-end traverse covers some 750 miles of rough open country. The harsh desert and slickrock are decidedly not for the uninitiated or the fainthearted. I'd certainly never dream of undertaking even a week out there, much less the months required for this trek.

I've been down the river on raft trips three times, so I could trace their progress from location to location even without subtitles. Seeing a different perspective on Lee's Ferry, the Boulder Canyon Dam site, the Little Colorado, Owl Eyes, and Havasu was fascinating.

The film also covers controversies from recent years about proposed development within the park and natural resource exploitation.

One question left unanswered: How did those dudes ferry themselves across the river at key junctures?

Regardless: what a magic evening. Sheesh. Ridiculous.

As I have written:

> In my dreams I wander high wastes
> Far from paths seldom trod
> The wind whips at my cheek
> Or at my back
> The sun is strong and the air cool
> The treeline a hundred feet below

And my feet lead me
Past ledges
Over domes
At the foot of an escarpment

Yes, these are the good dreams
When my soul is at rest
I wake smiling and refreshed

I do not dream of gardens
Or landscapes of the lush
Verdant vacation spots
Certainly not city lights
Or feather beds

My escape is not the hearth
But the harsh
High desert
Slickrock scree
Alpine bluff
Granite fault
Ground frost-free
But five score days each year

A copse of flowering trees
Is just a gaudy gaol
To my night-time eye
Though nocturnal tours are inspired
By what my waking mind has known

Precious few of my daytime hours
Promise such sweet healing

I have been tutored
In the beauty of natural desolation

O that my soul would love
Its own landscape so well
That I would long to wake

The way I anticipate dreams

Maracci

Joanne Maracci lives on the upper reaches of Beaver Creek with her painter husband, Vern White.

I spend a good deal of time on Upper Beaver Creek, what with my frequent forays up Pipestone Canyon and visits to friends George and Candy North Hoksbergen, Christine Kendall and Jack Kienast, Craig and Jenni Lynn Pony, and Leslee Goodman.

But I really haven't known Joanne or Vern.

Their house is hard to miss, though, a Spanish-looking stuccoed and columned spread perched in the Pipestone foothills and mercifully spared by the Carlton Complex fire in 2014.

Heck, for that matter, Joanne and Vern are hard to miss in general. Vern is a mountain of a man, and his art is as big; Joanne is a ubiquitous presence in the Methow, between her jewelry and her role as the Show Committee chair for Confluence Gallery (among other volunteering).

Last Saturday, while shopping at the Methow Valley Farmers Market in Twisp for a belated wedding gift for a relative, I stopped by to look at Joanne's jewelry. I usually ask what's new and have always admired what Joanne crafts. On this day, I selected earrings for Misuk. I figured it was about time I bought something from JM!

I did not expect my next twenty-four hours to be filled with Joanne Maracci.

A few hours later, I arrived at Methow Valley Riding Unlimited's 25th Anniversary Juleps & Jodhpurs event... and what to my wondering eyes should appear but Joanne Maracci, hatted and bedecked in grand makeshift-Derby style, complete with improvised garbage-bag bustle. Spectacular.

She asked if she could share a table with me and others, and we set up shop at the rear of the large tent pitched on the grounds of Moccasin Lake Ranch. In long and engaging conversation that afternoon, sandwiched around desserts and a sprawling and free-wheeling cross-country croquet match (Joanne's team finished well ahead of Lynette Westendorf and I!), I was greatly surprised to find that Joanne, Vern, and I most likely crossed paths much earlier this century. (Yes, I am old enough to say things like that.)

Like me, Joanne and Vern are "refugees" from "the Coast." They also lived for an extended period of time in the Seattle-area burb-ish city of Burien—and during the decade when my late wife, Jenn, and I lived there, Joanne and I were probably passing each other during walks around the pedestrian-friendly place.

When the seamier side of Burien got too much for them, however, they evacuated to the refuge provided by Joanne's mother's place on Upper Beaver during her mother's decline. I, meanwhile, did my caregiving in Des Moines as Jenn and I spent our final years together.

Joanne was greatly interested in hearing about my past association with the Okanogan—the years I spent researching, writing, producing, and filming my sixty-minute Western *Who Shall Stand* (1989)—and my attempt, at that time, to purchase a hilltop cabin site near Wannacut Lake, west of Tonasket.

I told her that the film was up on YouTube, and she said she'd love to see it. I promised to email her a link. Early last Sunday afternoon, I made good on the threat. And again, I figured that was that, as many people profess interest in such things without really meaning it. Social courtesies and all.

Just over ninety minutes later—meaning that she had not only immediately received my e-mail and read it, but that she had also clicked through to YouTube—Joanne emailed me back.

"Thank you for sharing this and your story with me Greg! The flick was fun to watch and I enjoyed the 'making of' featurette."

I was pretty astounded, to tell you the truth. My own family doesn't even tend to pay attention to what I do. When virtual strangers pay attention, I take notice.

"The back story," Joanne continued, "and all the challenges makes it that much more fun to watch the film. I can completely appreciate the long drives and the rattler and wind issues. Ya'll were pretty hardy to brave the heat and the wildlife out there!"

"Dang," I replied. "I'm impressed that you actually watched. One of the things I absolutely love about the Methow is how people are genuinely interested in one another. People are still people, and we'll never get entirely away from superficiality—but this place really has something special going for it."

Something really special.

Such as "a bit goofy" people like Joanne Maracci. (Her description, not mine!)

> Thank you again for sharing this, and it was nice getting to know you a little better yesterday. ~JM

∎

Crispy Bats

"Smells like crispy bats," announced Katie Suter as I walked into Winthrop Friendship Alliance Church yesterday morning.

"Crispy bats?" queried I.

"Crispy bats," quoth she, acting as if it were the most common combination of words on the planet. Of course, she does work at Trail's End Bookstore, so that might explain a thing or two.

In any event, "crispy bats" is not a phrase one expects to be greeted with at 8:35 on a frosty morning, whether one is walking into a church or some bar in a two-bit joke. Fortunately, pastor Jason Suter was on hand to explain.

"Some bats have been roosting under the entry floorboards to stay warm. We cranked up the heater in there this morning, and things started smelling a little roasty."

Ah. Crispy bats. I mentioned that I liked the sound of that. "Sounds like there might be a poem coming," offered Katie. Or a Wonderstruck, I rejoined.

And here we are.

I was reminded of many other close encounters I've had with not-so-crispy bats of various sizes and brands, not the least of which was a sweltering afternoon I spent on the "Adventure Tour" of Capricorn Caves outside Rockhampton on Australia's Gold Coast. "Adventure Tour" my backside. It was basically Death Crawl 1997.

A wiry Aussie buck about half my weight blithely led (I will not use the word "guided") my buddy David Stark and me through obstacles labeled Fat Man's Folly, Belly of the Whale, and Rebirth Canal. It was beyond this latter passage that I learned that my only recourse for survival was to essentially worm my way uphill "back into the womb," as it were, and I nearly suffered the hyperventilation fate featured at the crux of the horror film *The Descent*, if you've ever seen that nightmare.

Our oblivious guide nearly killed the two of us several times on that little adventure, but perhaps the worst part of the whole experience was the vitreous combination of perspiration and bat guano with which we became enslimed. In some passages, we were hands-and-kneeing it through four inches of powdered bat poop... with no protective clothing, no surgical masks, and dimly flickering headlamps.

"Enjoy a rewarding finish," the tour description states, "climbing to the surface ridge for panoramic views and cool breezes." Never mind the fact that, while you nearly fall to your death on the limestone karst three times while scaling this precipicial ridge in 98% humidity at 98 degrees Fahrenheit, you are covered from head to foot in about an inch and a half of guano mud... or that, having attained said "rewarding finish," your guide announces that this is simply the turnaround point. Yet another hour-plus of death-tempting treats in the blackness below awaits!

I opted out of this insanity and elected to forage my own Outback route overland to the visitor's center, itself festively adorned with thirty-pound fruit bats.

Dave arrived forty-five minutes later than did I, and he was literally dazed, having sprained an ankle leaping across a bottomless chasm onto a narrow ledge. The two of us were completely shell-shocked.

And it's not like we were adventure rookies. No. We were seasoned spelunkers. But these Aussies were what might be impolitely (but appropriately) describe as "bat-shit crazy."

A couple of days later, as we cruised above white Gold Coast beaches in an open-cockpit biplane and looked down on schools of thirty to fifty sharks basking in the shoals while surfers frolicked less than a mile away, I reflected that some stereotypes are deserved.

I have not been back to Australia since, and I have absolutely zero photos of that spelunking foray. Apparently, I should be glad. As I browsed through Capricorn Caves' Facebook photos today, I got a supe-queasy feeling in my stomach.

Yes, I've gotten plenty of storytelling mileage out of that visit… but I have still not recovered from the experience.

I do have the T-shirt, though… the complimentary one that reads, "I Survived Capricorn Caves."

Maybe I should burn it to help keep the church-bats warm this winter. Crispy bats, indeed.

Varn

Penelope and I were friends before we even met.

Almost exactly a year ago, Christine Kendall introduced me to Loy Young, Chair of the Confluence Gallery in Twisp, and before I had attended a single meeting of the Gallery board, fellow board member Penelope Evans Varn had sought me out on Facebook and friended me.

The affinity was natural. Penelope is a career editor and word nerd, and I had publicly established my own facility with language upon my arrival in Twisp late in 2018. If one looks me up on the Internet, one had best be prepared for an avalanche of verbiage.

Penelope is a remarkable woman. You can tell that she is because I remarked upon the fact.

Anybody who has spent much time around her knows that she is a whirling Dervish of energy, creativity, and wit who also has the uncanny ability to fall asleep at the drop of a hat. She is also the world's best chess player.

Let me explain. Whenever you get together to play chess with her you just end up in brilliant conversation for 2.5 hours without ever setting up the board. That's my kind of chess.

But the thing that I found most immediately remarkable about her was a keen insight into human psychology and behavior. The first time I had lunch with Penelope, she made observations about my personality traits that would have a profound impact on how my 2019 played out. This only happens via an amazing communication skill set. And I do mean amazing. Penelope's ability to listen well has left me consistently wonderstruck. Speechless, even.

I have not commented upon this to anybody. Not even her. I finally had to write about it because of a wildly entertaining exchange on Facebook this week.

"I would like every single person reading this," she posted on her timeline, "to stop using the word 'AMAZING' for 24 hours, and then when you resume using this horrifically overused word, I would like you to take note of all the ways you use it.

"If you apply this word to anything that does not literally—not figuratively—leave you speechless, then please choose another adjective. Thank you."

Oh, the irony. To have been rendered speechless—for months—by Penelope's communication skills and powers of perception, only to be temporarily constrained in use of the word which best applies.

The banter between Penelope and her friends about the topic was highly entertaining and lasted nearly two days. Being naturally sympathetic to Penelope's appeal for lexical restraint, I have done my best to comply with her request; and having considered things for more than twice her recommended period of moratorium, I last night determined that I should, today, employ the word in question in a sober and appropriate fashion.

Having done so above, and without further thrashing that already moribund horse, I will remark only two things further.

First, I am also wonderstruck by Penelope's curatorial abilities. I have been delighted to work with her and Friends of The Winthrop Public Library's Jill Volberding Sheley in preparing a series of literary events for the "Color of Words" show opening Saturday night at the Gallery, a show which Penelope has curated. I look forward to several weeks of art and related verbal wit.

Second, to steal Christine's comment from the aforementioned banter on Penelope's timeline this week...

Zing.

■

Sacrifice

A birdhouse hangs in the golden locust tree outside my home office window.

This spring, it has hosted a number of bird families. As the snow was still melting, eight or more chickadees shared it. Then a pair of juncoes. Then nuthatches. Most recently, it has been occupied by blue-gray gnatcatchers.

As the locust has started to leaf, one of the local squirrels has also been busy in the branches, harvesting, I suppose, little bits of goodies that get pushed out by emerging buds. The gnatcatchers have been none too happy with the squirrel's activity in the vicinity of their home.

On Thursday morning, I watched one of the gnatcatchers chasing the squirrel furiously around the tree.

Have you ever seen squirrels chase each other? Then you know how fast one of those suckers can move through the branches, and at all angles. The gnatcatcher was, to my surprise, having no trouble sticking with the squirrel, harassing him mercilessly with its beak and almost beating him with its wings.

Late Friday morning, I walked into my office to grab my phone and wallet before heading to The Iron Horse for curbside-business hours—and I witnessed the most astonishing thing.

Two gnatcatchers perched on a short dead branch just a few inches from the entrance to the birdhouse.

One of them leaned backward from the branch, its wings spread wide, white chest bare and bared, head back, beak jutting upward.

Three or four feet above, the squirrel sat watching.

Even before the squirrel struck, in that terrible momentary tableau, I sensed in the gnatcatcher's posture a challenge… and a sacrificial gesture. As if peace could only be won through surrender.

Why attribute such a motive to a bird? It's not as if they are sensitive sentient beings capable of such nobility and sentiment, right?

But last fall, I witnessed a sparrow literally push a finch out of the path of an attacking cat—just in the nick of time, and at its own peril.

The tom had sparrow for breakfast that day instead of the finch.

My late wife, Jenn, too, told stories of the hens and ducks around which she was raised—of the avian mothers mourning their lost chicks and frantic behavior if one of them should be in danger.

Birds understand a great deal about what goes on around them and do exhibit what we call emotion and altruism. Ravens and crows are known to remember specific people, and their behavior, for years.

So I was right in perceiving something extraordinary about to happen. That gnatcatcher's gesture was both meaningful and deliberate.

And the squirrel read it that way, too.

Still, I was extraordinarily dismayed when the squirrel struck and when the gnatcatcher gave itself up. Surely the bird's reflexes were sufficient to avoid the leaping squirrel; surely the vegetarian mammal had no cause to take a bird in its teeth.

Never had I seen a squirrel, most mischievous of rodents, attack or kill a bird.

Yet mere seconds later, there the squirrel sat in the neighboring fir with the gnatcatcher in its maw, staring at me as if to say, "Yeah? What's it to you?"

I yelled furiously at the squirrel through the window while the gnatcatcher's mate flitted frantically about in front of the birdhouse.

Misuk came running.

I dashed outside and grabbed the pressurized garden hose along the wall, directing a blast at the squirrel. He dropped the lifeless gnatcatcher and fled high into the locust. But he could not evade the stream of water. It chased him along the fence line and into the pines. I then picked up the hose by the garden gate and blasted the squirrel high into the ponderosa.

Two or three other gnatcatchers have joined the one who lost its mate. I have not seen the squirrel since. I don't know if my intervention with the hose played a role, but peace seems to have been achieved in the locust outside my window.

Was the gnatcatcher atoning for its earlier harassment of the squirrel?

Was it making a peace offering for an offensive mate?

Am I reading way too much into this May skirmish in the budding trees? I have no idea. But I have discovered that the squirrel was nesting somewhere very near the locust.

Still, I can't get the image of that gnatcatcher's outstretched wings out of my head. And I wonder: Perhaps the bird, in that moment, was thinking something along the lines of, "Forgive him, father, for the squirrel knows not what he is about to do."

Nothing would surprise me… because *everything* is so surprising.

■

Zoe

I do not work eight hours a day, seven days a week at The Iron Horse in Winthrop.

As co-owners of a mom-and-pop business, and with the constraints of Covid-19 fiscal insecurity, Misuk and I nonetheless keep the doors open daily, splitting shifts in a fairly random sort of way. Sometimes we are both in the shop from 10:00 AM to 6:00 PM on peak traffic days... but for the most part, it's one of us at a time.

On one relatively quiet Saturday afternoon, I was in the shop for just an hour or so to relieve Misuk when a couple of girls came in to browse for gifts and, I presumed, girly things. They made a sort of counter-clockwise tour through the aisles.

On their way out past the cash register, one of the masked girls looked up and rather startledly said, "I think I know you!"

I was taken aback. I do not know many fourteen-year-olds, and face coverings make it difficult to identify the few that I do know... barring distinctive hairstyles, piercings, or tats.

"Well, where are you from?" I inquired.

"Federal Way," she replied.

Without many more words, I discovered that this was not a fourteen-year-old girl at all, but a young adult artist named Zoe Prince.

I know her, and her family, quite well! She in fact created monarch butterfly artwork as a hospice gift for my late wife, Jenn, artwork which I later used (with Zoe's permission, of course!) on the cover of *Taking Flight*, Jenn's volume of collected poems. I was able to point to Zoe's artwork proudly displayed on our "local authors" counter.

The following day, a group of Zoe's friends came by to admire the butterfly.

Elvis Costello once remarked in response to a critic's query about the meaning of his lyrics, "If I could say it differently, I would have written a different song." Zoe created her image of a butterfly in response to a plea I sent out for notes of encouragement to my dying wife. True to her instincts as an artist, and knowing of the role that a butterfly had played in Jenn's deliverance from years of pain and torment and guilt, Zoe responded with her heart and a gift that spoke more than words possibly could.

Jenn did not have long to cherish that gift, but cherish it she did.

Art is communication; and by and large, visual art is created by souls for whom verbal art is either impossible or simply not the best way to express what needs to be expressed. Even writers must choose: Poem? Essay? Novel? Graffiti?

And then, for all artists, and in the vein of Costello's remark: Because a work of art is neither didactic nor clinical in aim, what do we do with the response to our art? Artists desire to communicate something specific, if indirectly; and ultimately, they desire a reaction to that communication.

But for the vast majority of artists, and for the vast majority of their creation: crickets. There are very few Rowlings, Picassos, Coppolas, or Arbusae.

Zoe has herself mused on the artist's dilemma in an unpublished essay.

"There's a certain apprehension that comes with revealing your artwork to someone," she writes, "an anxiety that they won't like it on a basic level, that their immediate reaction will be confusion or uncertainty.

"That anxiety is hardly ever well founded because hardly ever will someone tell you they don't like what you've created."

Yes.

Not only crickets, but an even more intense silence when the response is negative… or confused. She continues:

> Even when people appreciate your work on the surface level and the affirmation is almost enough to fuel another creation, there's always a hunger for someone to understand the work that you've put into the creation… see the detail in the upper corner, or the way that the lines converge just right, or the way that smudge or empty space made the slightest difference in perfectly capturing someone's likeness.

So it's not just communication of ideas; it's also communication of process:

> Finding someone who can fully appreciate your work is one of the most important and necessary tools an artist can have, because while the anxiety of showing a piece to someone who can see into the dark corners of it much surpasses the anxiety of showing a piece to your glaucomatous grandmother, or anyone else of that caliber, the relief of a positive reaction from a more critical audience is enough to fuel further creations and improvements thereupon.

And so we find that Zoe is not only masterful with pencil and brush, she also has a distinctive way with words.

"The relief that someone can really see specifically what it was you did," she concludes, "or even what you intended to do never ceases to put a smile on my face."

And then her thoughts become transcendent: seeing that creative bent from a divine point of view... applying those very same principles to a universe that longs for us to see specifically and wonderfully what it has done for us and what it intends for us.

Be wonderstruck by all the art around you, whether created by women and men or by the hand of nature and God.

Put a smile on the face of the universe.

■

Pelotonia

As I entered the Washington Pass viewpoint turnout on Wednesday afternoon, I noticed a couple of cyclists snapping photos of each other in front of the pass signage.

That's a wicked climb, from either side of the pass, and I knew it must have been a big deal for the dudes. I pulled over to the shoulder and offered to take a photo of the two of them together. They were grateful for the offer and accepted.

From a comfortably social distance, I asked which side they had ascended. Impressively, they had come up the Skagit side!

Since they were in the neighborhood, I recommended that they visit the viewpoint, as it really is quite spectacular… The younger of the two asked how far it was, and I said I thought it was a quarter mile. (I didn't really know, but I've walked it in the snow, and that's about how far it felt.) And then I said my goodbyes and drove to the viewpoint for a snack break.

For whatever reason, I walked the loop trail clockwise. I've been there several times and usually do the typical tourist route: counterclockwise to the granite-slab overlook and then continuing around to return to the parking area.

Halfway around the afternoon's clockwise loop, I stopped for a packet of Sun Chips. By the time I got to the overlook, the two cyclists were also preparing to depart.

"Are you annoyed with me?" I asked the younger of the two, who was closest to me.

"A little!" he replied. "It was eight-tenths of a mile, not a quarter."

We laughed and chatted about the view and the difficulties of estimating distances on foot. When I asked if they were headed back down the Skagit side, I learned that Blaine and Logan were not just out for a grueling idle tour of the North Cascades. No. They were on Day 6 of a three-and-a-half-month cross-country trek as part of "Pelotonia Across America."

From the explanatory postcards Blaine carries: "Pelotonia started out as a 3-day bicycle event to raise funds for The James Center Hospital and Solove Research Institute at The Ohio State University... To date, over $210,000,000 has been raised."

Blaine, with sons Logan and Levi, has participated for the last twelve years. He is a three-time cancer survivor himself and lost his wife, Cheryl, to cancer in 2012. The family takes this effort quite personally, and in the wake of the Covid-19 shutdown they came up with their own unique "MyPelotonia" challenge: biking from the tip of the Olympic Peninsula to the Atlantic coast in Delaware.

Logan and Blaine are riding, while Levi handles logistical support. I gave them tips on camping and dining in Winthrop (nothing better than take-out East 20 Pizza after a long ride!) and they were kind enough to visit me at The Iron Horse on their way out of town late yesterday morning.

"I didn't expect to see you," I told Blaine as he and Logan were preparing to mount up for their Day 7 trip over the Loup to Okanogan.

"Because it's so late in the day?" he asked.

I nodded.

"Yeah, we prefer to wait until the temperature hits 100 before we start our ride," he cracked.

These dudes are serious. Wonderstruck!

■

Shekels

I stood at the counter of The Iron Horse, a 2-shekel Israeli coin in my hand, mouth hanging open, as the giver of the coin left the shop. I didn't even catch his name.

Not just wonderstruck; dumbstruck.

I hope I have been clear in these Wonderstruck essays: I am shamelessly dedicated to the proposition that "great apparent coincidences" are not meaningless, as Chistopher Hitchens argued, but "only occur to the intellect that has rehearsed and prepared for them"—to steal Hitchens' own words, which he meant as a criticism, not as a compliment.

I do rehearse and prepare my mind to find great meaning in what the universe dishes out. Absolutely. I find it's a much better way to live than rehearsing and preparing my mind for meaninglessness—to completely ignore what the universe is dishing out and instead pursue my own short-sighted agendas.

Been there. Done that. Burned the t-shirt.

When God goes to the trouble of interrupting my day, I find it very worthwhile to turn that interruption into Plan A. So holding that 2-shekel coin in my hand was the sign that God had gone to great lengths to arrange an interruption.

Where was that going? I didn't know yet. But I knew it was going somewhere.

To backtrack: The previous day, a thirty-something traveler and his friend had stopped into The Iron Horse. They were not there to shop, however. They were seeking information.

First, the young man asked if I could recommend a free place to pitch a tent for the night. Given my familiarity with the roads and the trails of the local National Forest lands, being helpful on that score wasn't all that difficult.

Several minutes later, the young man returned to ask further about where they might purchase some good beef for a cookout. Again, I was not put out by recommending Thomson's Custom Meats at Thriftway.

The next morning, the traveler returned to the shop, this time without his companion. When he brought a small memento to the counter for purchase, I asked how his campout and meal had been, and a short conversation ensued.

Somehow, the conversation turned to his heritage. I had gleaned that he was not born in the United States and also learned that he was an Israeli who had been living and working in the Seattle area for fourteen years. As we concluded our chat and our credit-card transaction, he slid a shiny coin across the counter toward me.

"What's that?" I asked. It was clearly not U.S. currency.

"It's a shekel," he replied.

"It's been a while since you've been in Israel," I observed. "Why are you carrying Israeli coins?"

"A friend gave them to me as a challenge," came the answer.

I knew what that meant, without further explanation, and I picked up the coin to examine it.

"The shekel—wasn't that the coin used to pay the temple tax?" I was referencing Matthew 17, when Jesus directed Peter to find a shekel in the mouth of a fish.

"That's right," the stranger replied. "Only this is the 'New Sheqel,' and it's a 2-shekel piece." And he turned and left as my jaw gaped open.

To back up a few days further: I had been inspired to write a poem about the shekel in the fish's mouth, that passage of Scripture in Matthew 17. I had not yet published the piece, despite having workshopped the poem with Confluence Poets that Monday. I was still mulling it over in my mind.

How often in fifty-seven years does one spend a week mulling over a shekel in the mouth of a fish? How often in fifty-seven years does one have a stranger slide a shekel over the counter and report that it's a challenge coin? How often in fifty-seven years do those two things happen *in the same week*?

For those who don't know: "A challenge coin may be a small coin or medallion, bearing an organization's insignia or emblem and carried by the organization's members. Traditionally, they might be given to prove membership when challenged and to enhance morale. In addition, they are also collected by service members and law enforcement personnel."

The Wikipedia article states that a bit weakly. Challenge coins are rarely given to "civilians" by soldiers and first responders; when they are, it is a sign of great respect.

What had I done for this stranger to earn such respect? I never got the chance to ask, and only he knows for sure. But I was sure wonderstruck by the timing of receiving that 2-shekel challenge coin.

How do I know about challenge coins?

My late wife, Jenn, was given one by an Air Force veteran in Scotland after a long conversation with him just a couple months before she died. I was reminded of that later that evening as I was doing my Bible study with Misuk. I suddenly recalled ex-Ranger Ken Mesler explaining the significance of challenge coins to me upon our return from Scotland in 2017.

"You can be assured," Ken said, "that it's a great honor."

And just as suddenly came the thought, "You need to call Ken."

I did.

"Ken, is there something we can be praying about for you?" I asked without preamble.

Ken did not hesitate in his reply, nor did he ask why I had called out of the blue for the first time in a year. There was indeed reason for prayer.

Sometimes you just take what the universe slides across the counter. You don't ask why.

Wonderstruck.

Pirateer

I was introduced to Pirateer by my nephew, Jacob Rosok—many moons ago now, when he was just eight years old.

During the 1990s (and even into the early years of the new millennium) I spent a good deal of time gaming with my sister, Elane, and her family. One of Jacob's and Emily's favorites was this simple scalawag board game.

The objective: Sail your fleet of three ships from your home pirate port, grab the treasure from the central island, and return with it safely to your home port. Along the way, you may sink your opponents' ships or get hit by a hurricane (in a favored game variation). Ships navigate to rolls of the dice along a grid overlaid on the board's map, or via "trade winds" which allow diagonal travel along the grid.

During the long illness of my late wife, Jenn, we acquired literally dozens of games and played them all with great regularity. Pirateer was one of our earliest acquisitions, and the box shows signs of its heavy use.

Personally, I favor the game for the reason I prefer most of my faves: You can teach someone the game without the use of a rule book, and in about three minutes. The explanation is as long as that hefty paragraph above, with a couple added sentences. You can invite friends over for a game night and get to playing almost immediately.

And for such a simple game—and as is the case with a lot of simple games—the play is consistently surprising and engaging. As one prominent reviewer noted, it can be addictive. Most often you can complete a game in twenty minutes or so, depending on the variation you choose, and so can squeeze in a mini-tournament over the course of an evening.

As I have cut down my game repertoire over my last two moves since Jenn passed away, Pirateer is now one of only about a dozen that I have kept. And I'm glad I have!

The game has now been out of production for about a dozen years. You can still pick up a used one on eBay relatively cheaply, but I don't expect that to be true much longer.

Misuk did not come to our marriage with a history of gaming. She was familiar with the handful of traditional Korean board games from her childhood, but during her decades in the United States, she was not introduced to much outside Bunco.

Pirateer was one of the obvious choices for quick integration into our married life… and Misuk has become a Pirateer fanatic! She is absolutely cutthroat and has mastered all the intricacies of pirate navigation via grids. In fact, in all my decades of Pirateer, I had not seen one of her favorite tactics: the blockage of an opponent's port by sinking a ship in the harbor. The move has now become a staple of our matches.

We favor a variation in which we each play two fleets of ships as allies… so blocking one port still gives the remaining ships a port to which to return.

As our friendship was forming, Misuk asked about my fascination with game-playing. I told her that it was not just a pleasantly social way to pass time with friends; many of my life's greatest lessons have been formed from game-playing.

Like with pinball: You can't lose your composure over what happens with the first ball; the final ball can make all the difference, and your mind has to be ready to take advantage when the opportunity comes—eyes on the prize.

Or being badly behind at Pinochle: Yes, the odds may not look good; but if you play your cards right, you always have a chance to "shoot the moon"—and coming back from the dead over the course of three hours is far more legendary than winning a quick three-hand victory.

For my birthday the other day, we packed the Pirateer board into a secluded shady spot along Cutthroat Creek and played a short three-game mini-tournament.

We split the first two games, and the third was shaping up to be a blowout in Misuk's favor. Up four ships to two, Misuk had blocked both of my ports, grabbed the treasure from the island, and was just two spaces from entering her port. I managed to navigate one of my remaining boats to a position with a direct line of attack just three spaces away at the end of my turn.

Misuk's next roll of the dice gave her two options: She could use a two to move to the mouth of her home port, then a one to move into the safety of her port passage, just three spaces from anchorage… or she could use the one and the two to sail away from port and sink my sitting duck. She chose the latter.

Suffice to say that I mounted one of the most amazing comebacks in naval history, eliminating her remaining four-ship fleet with my sole remaining vessel. I could not return to port; but I was the last pirate standing, and I had the treasure.

Misuk's life lesson for the day: *Ignore the enemy. Just do what you need to do.*

Wonderstruck. Such good, good life advice for any time—but especially for the duration of Covid.

■

Bullion

I met a friend for lunch at La Fonda not long ago. With her she brought a 1930s tin breadbox loaded with old coins—about thirty pounds, mostly wheat pennies and "collectible" coin sets.

"I'm seriously considering tossing this in the dumpster," she said. "It's been passed through who knows how many hands before I inherited it, and I can't imagine there's anything of value in here."

"You're probably right," I agreed.

But I nonetheless did a quick sort through the breadbox contents. She had come to me for help, knowing that I have some knowledge of the rough value of old coins.

As we both suspected, the coins had been well sifted by others. The things collectors look for right off—silver, mostly—were almost completely absent. Just lots of odd little boxes almost overflowing with pennies, tourist replicas, sealed plastic cases of perfectly ordinary coins, and one opaque tube with a few small coins sealed with very old and crusty packing tape.

I reloaded the breadbox and told my friend the most likely fate for the collection: sold for a pittance to a coin or pawn broker, who would then turn the collection around to a coin dealer who would sift the collection for any potential valuables and sell those for an immense profit.

I did advise against the dumpster option.

As a parting thought, I said, "There are some Indian head pennies and buffalo nickels that we could sell at The Iron Horse. I'd be happy to give you bulk market value for those."

"Well, why don't you take the whole lot and sort those out, then?" she suggested.

As I happened to have a free evening I set to sorting the collection immediately upon arriving home. The Indian heads and buffaloes went into a separate box as I handled every coin in that thirty-pound tin… and then I came to that small sealed tube.

I peeled away the crusty packing tape, popped the top off the tube, and was surprised to find that most of it was filled with old packing material, which I pulled from the tube's opening.

And what to my wondering eyes should appear when I spilled the ten coins from that tube into my palm… but shining gold!

Swiss franc bullion dated between 1902 and 1947, the legacy of some relative's forgotten sojourn in post-war Europe.

Overlooked treasure in the corner of a 1930s breadbox.

Some $4000 that almost found its way from Switzerland into an Okanogan County landfill.

I made a very excited phone call to my friend with some very, very good news.

"I have found that humanity is not incidentally engaged, but eternally and systematically engaged," wrote G. K. Chesterton, "in throwing gold into the gutter and diamonds into the sea."

Oh, very much yes.

Wonderstruck.

(The name of this friend has been withheld because, well, you know.)

■

Kaileah Akker

If you spend much time in Twisp, you are familiar with Kaileah Akker... whether you know it or not.

I first met Kaileah the afternoon of 2019's Trashion Show.

A third-generation Methow Valley resident, Kaileah was raised in the Tri-cities area and moved permanently to the Methow the summer of 2018 after completing her college education. While I landed in Twisp about that same time and quickly became immersed in The Confluence and the Methow Valley Community Center, Kaileah took up residence in Winthrop with her grandmother Eleanor and loomed large as a volunteer firefighter and as a barista at The Rocking Horse, where her height, hair, smile, and consistently positive buzz of energy quickly made her fast friends with a vast number of locals.

I had volunteered to coordinate the security team at the 19th Annual Trashion Show. For those not familiar with the wildly popular Methow tradition, Trashion is a rowdy, tipsy, and often bawdy sendup of fashion runway shows which requires that all styles modeled be made entirely of recycled/repurposed trash. The event has been a staple fundraiser for the art programs of The Confluence.

The 19th edition presented a unique challenge. In 2018, the tipsiness had slopped over into some underage attendees, which threatened the future of the show due to liability issues. For 2019, Trashion was re-cast as a 21-and-over-only event. This meant a broadly expanded charter for the security team, which would need to card every attendee and monitor the handling of booze amidst the inflow and egress of attendees to and from the MVCC gymnasium. You never know, after all, when a Liquor Board rep will appear.

To greatly expand the muscle of the security team, Lindsey Bryson recruited the Methow volunteer firefighters and put them under my direction. Most attended the orientation the day before the event, but one was unable to attend due to work responsibilities. That was Kaileah. "It's pronounced 'kay-LEE-uh,'" her very protective comrades informed me.

The day of the event, the security team met early to divide up into the shifts that would cover ticketing check-in (the ID detail), the outdoor lounge for ticketed guests, the side entrance (and most likely avenue for illicit booze), balcony access, and booze-checking at the gymnasium doors.

Is it possible to instantly bond with a person thirty-five years your junior? Apparently so.

I can tell you that Kaileah was not at all what I was expecting. At 6' 2", she was right at my eye level. Exceedingly comfortable in her own skin, she was neither trying to leverage her size into some macho competition with her fellows nor overplaying the femininity of her physique. Her long tenure in the spotlight as middle blocker in high school and collegiate volleyball had apparently simply taught her: You're going to notice me, whether I like it or not... so I might as well accept that I am noticeable, and make the most of it. Many tall women seem to shrink from their height, but Kaileah added to hers with flamboyant locks of colored hair, moderate piercings, and a directness that, to some, was probably unsettling or intimidating.

But what stood out to me that long evening was how Kaileah stood her ground.

The new security policies for Trashion Show were not popular. While tensions eased once the booze and fashions started flowing, the early hours were not pleasant. Some guests arrived from Mazama without their IDs, while some elderly guests assumed that their age alone provided sufficient ID. Some guests just naturally objected to being corralled in various places in sweltering temperatures for varying lengths of time. Most just found the amount of attention being paid to the location of their liquor cups ludicrous.

Now, volunteer firefighters are used to being universally loved and are really very easygoing. When they suddenly became the focus of ire from fun-loving partiers, well... let's just say the sheen of the gig quickly faded. They, too, wanted a little fun out of the evening. By the time the show was hitting its stride, the majority of the team was begging off duty. But not Kaileah. No, this 22-year-old was "kicking ass and taking names," as the Urban Dictionary says, "the act of being unequivocally awesome."

Over the course of several hours, and often working literally shoulder to shoulder, I found in Kaileah an old soul and kindred spirit. Once the after-party started and Kaileah finally filtered off to dance with "her peeps," the implication was clear. I was one of her people, too, despite the multigenerational gap between us and my disinclination, in the moment, to also dance.

But that really says little about me. Kaileah readily talks about her *reiki*, the attention she pays to her spiritual energy and how it affects the health of her body, her friends, and her community. If you respond at all to positive spiritual energy, Kaileah's will pour into you and feed off of yours in a classic application of the scientific principles of Systems Theory.

If our individuality is but an illusion, nonetheless useful as metaphor and pragmatism, and if we are all really highly interconnected at the cellular level, then it's no surprise that a spiritually aware being such as Kaileah Akker can have such a positive influence on a community… perhaps, even, simply mirroring the connectedness of a community that already exists.

By early 2020, when I heard the news that Confluence Executive Director Sarah Jo Lightner had hired Kaileah to join the Confluence staff, I literally jumped out of my chair, pumped my fists in the air, and shouted, "Yessss!!!" I knew that some Methow non-profit was going to snap this youngster up and was thrilled that The Confluence made the move first. And I am beyond pleased that, when Sarah Jo migrated to Methow Recycles, I was on the Confluence board which officially made Kaileah Akker its Executive Director.

The leadership she has exhibited throughout this pandemic has been almost ridiculously valuable. Along with Lindsey Bryson, Sharla Lynn, Amanda Jackson Mott, Jamie Pettito, Rebecca Gallivan, and others, Kaileah has made the most of the opportunities for bringing the community together in the face of a pandemic. Frankly, the fall Art Walk and Mistletoe Madness were the best community gatherings of which I have ever been a part. And I'm an old codger.

Kaileah Akker knows who she is and where she stands, and she stands her ground. She is your Middle Blocker for All Seasons. She is also my friend and frequent backcountry companion.

She is a blessing.

■

Epona Rose

Does Epona Rose seek to be a goddess?

Perhaps. But what she really wants right now is pretty simple: to find a place for herself and her son to live.

Rainan Marrow, Epona's son, suffers from spinal muscular atrophy (SMA), an incurable gene-based disease that keeps him so weak that he cannot walk or function well on his own. With such special needs, he and Epona require an especially accessible living space. If you reside in the Methow, you know that such homes are in critically short supply.

And if you live in the Methow, the odds are that you are familiar with Epona and Rainan, Rainan's father Alexander Heathen, and many of their friends. You may have read about them in the *Methow Valley News* last year when County health officials shut down their sustainable-living community off Poorman Creek, allowing only Alex and his immediate household to remain. Just before winter, this threw Epona and others out of their yurts, tents, and simple cabins mostly onto the goodwill of friends and neighbors. When you live off the land and you lose that land, you don't have much of a living left.

While at the Heathen enclave, Epona was indeed something of a goddess-mama. Personally, I think she still is. I treasure the opportunity to be in her company. She takes her name from a Roman-goddess protector of equine species, and, after the fashion of many Greco-Roman deities, she has been closely associated with the land. Quite by choice. Berkeley-educated, and under the tutelage of Vilden Lynx, Epona deliberately partnered with Alex, Harmony Cronin, Joshua Dodds, Katie Rose, Tatterhawk, Taylor Rap, and others in an attempt to live in harmony and peace with the land, taking no more from it than it willingly gives—respectfully and gratefully so—and treading lightly on the land so as to leave, as it were, the most minuscule of footprints.

I know this from experience: When your aims are idealistic, the realities of extreme medical conditions can bring your dreams crashing down pretty hard. I am fairly certain that Epona and Alex did not foresee the countless visits to medical professionals, the endless hours of diagnostics and consultations to yield such an obscure diagnosis for Rainan as SMA, or the high-tech wheelchair necessary for their son's mobility and comfort. I have spent enough time at Poorman Creek, Skalitude, and primitive skills gatherings to know that Epona and her friends live very simply and with a very low profile. The transition away from Poorman Creek and into Winthrop as a townie cannot have been easy for Epona.

Nor can the need for reaching out for help to the larger community. Some might say it's "humbling." Others might find it humiliating. Epona has found it necessary.

As a pastor, I often have people ask, "What can I do about things like Russia invading Ukraine or protesters dying in Myanmar?"

And this is always one righteous answer: "Help those near at hand."

Some might call it one exponent of "The Butterfly Effect." One philosophy likens it to the ripples cast from a single falling stone. Agrarian metaphor talks about the sowing of seeds. Pop lyrics from the '70s say, "Love the one you're with." Making your immediate community better always makes the world better.

And Epona always, always strives to make this community—and the world—a better place to live.

Consider responding in kind, and helping others in their time of need!

■

Panties

...and then there was the hitchhiker in his panties.

You should know that Misuk has not learned to distinguish women's underthings from men's. To her, they are all "panties," and she is most likely unaware that men prefer the terms underwear, shorts, skivvies, tighty-whiteys, boxers, undies, jockeys, drawers, loincloth... *anything* but the dreaded "panties." And it's important that you see this story from, sort of, her point of view.

So here was this guy on the shoulder of the road in his tight panties, thumb out, barefoot, kind of dancing like he had stepped out of the fire and into the frying pan. Which was actually not a bad metaphor for his predicament.

Misuk and I had made one of our periodic resupply trips to Omak and were on our way back to Winthrop. Coming down the steep grade to the Loup Loup Creek crossing, we could see a dark SUV parked in the pullout on the north side of Highway 20, right at the bottom of the grade where it crosses the creek.

Rather suddenly, a nearly naked figure dashed out from behind the SUV, not quite into the roadway, but close. It was the aforementioned Man in Panties.

Misuk's (perhaps correct) instinct was to recommend that I keep driving. After all, a dancing hitchhiker in panties is not exactly run of the mill for a drive over the Loup. Many things are, of course... like deer, cows, snowbanks, rolled-over cars, mudslides, and so on. Even the occasional elk or bear. But prancing panty-men? No.

I figured, however, as long as we kept our doors locked, I could dare a rolled-down window and a question or two. So I eased into the pullout alongside the dancer.

"Can you give me a lift into Winthrop?" he blurted.

Not likely, I thought.

"What seems to be the problem?" I asked instead. Other than dancing around the shoulder of the road nearly naked.

"I'm locked out of my car," was the less-than-explanatory reply.

And really... I generally have a low degree of confidence in the honesty of men in their panties in the middle of nowhere. How could I be sure it was his car? It's not like I could ask for ID.

I noticed he was not just nearly naked... He looked like he'd been herding kittens. While crawling amongst them, covered in bits of tuna. Bleeding, thin, long scratches everywhere. This was beginning to feel like an M. Night Shyamalan movie... but more hair-raising due to proximity—and with an unfortunately less-predictable outcome.

When I failed to respond in a timely manner, thanks to the various macabre scenarios playing out in my head, he finally figured he needed to explain a little more. He could see me dubiously eyeing his bleeding torso.

"I went up the canyon for a swim," he stammered, shivering a little. It had probably been warm enough for a dip a couple hours earlier, but now, just before dusk on a stormy July evening, the shady canyon was indeed getting cool.

"And then I heard all these wild animals!" he exclaimed, a little wild himself. "I just ran. All my clothes and my keys and wallet and phone are up the creek."

Yeah. And you along with them, I thought. *Without your paddle.*

Was this a creepy invitation to join the Man in Panties on an up-canyon jaunt to... bwa ha ha... "retrieve his keys"? I was not biting.

"Seriously," he said, knowing his tale sounded just a little fishy. "I live in Winthrop. I have spare keys at the house."

Ummm... yes. But you have no pants on. I do not fancy spending the next half hour within an arm's reach of you.

Here was the safe bet, and still compassionate. "Sounds like you need some professional help," I offered, not catching my own double meaning. "Let me call 911 for you." There are people out there equipped to help in situations like these, and with the requisite self-defense skills and such.

I pulled out my phone, but there was no coverage at the bottom of Loup Loup. Undaunted, I asserted, "Wait right here." As if he intended, perhaps, to rejoin the animals in his panties.

"I'll just drive back up to the top of the grade where's there's a signal."

And having left Panty Man just where he was but dancing a little less, I did precisely that. On the way back toward Winthrop, we slowed down enough to assure him that law enforcement was, indeed, on the way.

And with that, we exited this strange little drama, stage left.

I never checked the police blotter in the *Methow Valley News* to see how the 911 operator logged my report; but the next time I left home to drive solo over the Loup, Misuk stopped me on the way out the door.

"Watch for deer," came the usual reminder.

"And men in panties."

∎

The Methow

Have you ever had one of those absolutely magnificent and perfect weeks?

On Sunday afternoon during my lunch break, a jazz duo had staked out a busk on the steps of Winthrop's Town Hall; so instead of plunking my butt on the porch's bench (as is my wont) I plunked it on the neighboring stoop and sunned while the musicians strummed. After I ate, I thanked them for bringing some music to the streets, as buskers are oddly uncommon in Winthrop. I recommended some establishments which might let them play a few gigs while they were staying in town and went on my merrier way.

On Monday night, after completing my prep for the next four days of camping in the National Forest below Washington Pass, I had the most remarkable dream in which I rode a one-hundred-mile bicycle rally in the Alps. The dream was extraordinarily detailed, covering the several days of the rally (staged in twenty-five-mile segments), and I could feel every bump in my bum, the ache in my quads during the climbing stages, and the exhilaration of the downhill stage, which passed in a blur.

On Tuesday, Adam from Methow Motion collected me, Dave, and the Shy Pilot (and our gear) to deposit us at our unmarked trailhead off Highway 20. After weeks of cool temperatures and frequent rains, the weather finally turned to settled and dry as we wound our way through Winthrop and Mazama and threaded the edge of last year's Cedar Fire on the way up the Early Winters watershed. After unloading right on schedule (thank you, Adam!) we hauled and packed our gear to our destination at the old Survey Camp on the Peace Trail. We managed it all in just two trips! Then we rehabbed three tent sites, built a new fire pit directly on a massive granite slab, grabbed a very quick five-gallon bucket of water from the Cutthroat Cascades flood, and gathered an easy mountain of firewood. The Shy Pilot was soon prepping a marvelous open-fire forest feast: Korean short ribs, garlic mashed potatoes, and corn on the cob... with ribeye steaks for dessert!

To polish off the day, I reveled in the complete setup of my new backpacking rig: two-person tent, compact cot, and state-of-the-art inflatable pad. A most comfy camp!

On Wednesday, we slept late and for the afternoon I shared my Peace Trail rehab work with Dave and the Shy Pilot. For the last two summers I have worked on clearing the Cutthroat Spur and the segment of the old Early Winters Trail from the Cutthroat ford to the Early Winters ford. At the end of last season, my trail work had come up just two or three hundred yards short of the Early Winters ford, so the last bit was a little rough; and three trees came down right on the trail over the winter. Not exactly a walk through the park.

But at least you can now hike that stretch without the need for post-hike medical attention. We did a little additional clearing while we were out there, as I always walk that trail with a pruner, a folding saw, and a lopping axe. Upon our return from the ford, Dave prepped that evening's meal of

Johnsonville bratwursts (with freshly chopped onion) and Reser's potato salad. (I do love camping with an ice chest!)

Thursday, the weather was absolutely perfect. Forgoing breakfast, we packed a lunch and headed off to Cutthroat Lake... probably marking the first time in the last fifty years that anyone has hiked directly from the Early Winters Trail to Cutthroat Lake. (The opening of the North Cascades Highway in 1972 rendered the Early Winters Trail largely obsolete.) Under blue and cloudless skies, we enjoyed the scenery of the Cutthroat Trail while encountering hardly a soul. Once we reached the (broken-down) log bridge at the fork to the lake, the trail transitioned entirely to snow, leaving precious few places to sit and enjoy lunch in the sun. Fifteen- to twenty-foot cornices of snow and ice still clung to the ridge tops towering above the lake.

After enjoying the views, we retreated to the bridge for lunch and re-hydration. As the afternoon progressed and as we trailed back down the valley, we encountered dozens of hikers! It felt odd after just two days of relative isolation. For dinner that night I prepared ricotta and prosciutto tortellini with chunky vegetable pasta sauce... and the Shy Pilot contributed crispy fire-roasted garlic bread. As was the case the previous two nights, campfire talk revolved around politics, faith, and the many, many adventures the three of us have shared over the years.

Friday, Adam again collected us right on time from the shoulder of Highway 20 (thank you again, Adam!), and we returned to Winthrop where Misuk reported some most excellent news on a new business proposition. We were buying the Farmers Exchange Building in Winthrop! To celebrate, we treated Dave and the Shy Pilot to pulled pork at The Methow Valley Ciderhouse.

On Saturday, just before my lunch break, who should walk into The Iron Horse but the jazz buskers from the previous weekend? Dale and Shelley Lawrence invited me to stop by Confluence Park to hear their set before they finally left town; and so I grabbed my lunch, and did. After they played a couple of numbers, I was able to quiz them about their choice of instruments and mode of musical expression, a very enjoyable artistic discussion.

That was a fine tuneup for that evening, the closing performance of the (re-)annual Methow Valley Chamber Music Festival—suspended for two years due to Covid, and now enjoying a new venue at one of my favorite spots in the valley, Twisp Terrace Lodge (now Casia Lodge). Artistic Director Keven Krentz put together (and performed in) a dynamite program of Mozart, Tchaikovsky, and several twentieth-century and contemporary composers. The setting was elegant and intimate, with our seats less than twenty feet from the performers—and the finale of Tchaikovsky's *Piano Trio in A Minor, Opus 50* was set against the backdrop of the sun setting behind Mount Gardner and the North Cascades. Unreal, really.

What a privilege it is to live in a valley where the natural and human arts are both so fine, and so accessible.

What a week. Wonderstruck.

■

Lost & Found

And there my driver's license was, resting on the front steps.

What an odd place for it to show up! When I discovered that my wallet was missing the previous Thursday night, I was convinced that I had misplaced it somewhere inside the house. I had a very vague recollection of having pulled it out of my pocket and placing it somewhere unusual, with the intent of doing something with it sometime very soon… so I did a quick check in all the places I might ordinarily remove my wallet from my pocket: at the back door, in the walk-in closet, in the kitchen.

No luck.

So I ran through my memory banks to figure out when I last used my wallet, either to get cash or a credit card. As near as I could recollect, that had been almost two full days before, at Ace Hardware on Wednesday morning. I checked my credit card statements online, and, yep, I had last used my credit card at Ace.

So what had I done with my wallet over the last two days? Carrying that thing has become so second nature, and my wallet so progressively thin, that I am now rarely conscious of it at all… until I need it.

Or until I can't find it.

Which admittedly happens more frequently than it ought.

But I did have a strange feeling that something wasn't quite right when I returned to the trailhead with Terry L. Pisel Thursday evening. I had gone directly to the trailhead at 3:00 PM from work and had changed clothes alongside the road. Intending to stop at Three Fingered Jack's for dinner on the way home, I instinctively patted my pockets when we returned to the car... and no wallet. At that point, I just naturally presumed I had left it at home. Precedents and all.

So the search began in earnest when I got home after dinner. And it continued for two and a half hours, at which point Misuk came home from work and found the house upside down. And her husband very frustrated.

By Friday morning, with my backside due in Tacoma for my nephew's wedding reception that evening, I had written off my lost wallet. I figured it would turn up in the house at some point... but in the meantime, I needed to replace my credit cards and driver's license. And did so.

The weekend wore on, and by Monday I had mostly forgotten about my wallet.

At midday, I came home from The Iron Horse for a break and for some strange reason decided to sit in the sun on the patio outside our rec room.

I have done this approximately 3.5 times over the last three years.

And as I sat there in the sun, I noticed something sitting on our front porch.

I got up to investigate.

And, lo! there lay a handwritten note: "My name is Cory Heuer. I found drivers lic on Hwy 20. Any questions call." And there was a phone number.

And there was my driver's license and my Hank's member card!

What the heck…

In the first place… about 2.5 people have shown up at our door unannounced over the last three years, and that one of them should have found my driver's license was remarkable. But then: What about my credit cards? And the wallet itself, a treasured memento of my 2018 visit to Scotland? And *where* on Highway 20?

Boy, was I baffled. I called the number for more information, but the call went directly to voicemail. I checked credit card activity for fraud but found nothing. I racked my brain about where on Highway 20 I might have pulled my wallet from my pocket…

And then I thought: Maybe this Cory Heuer is on Facebook. And maybe I can scare him up on Messenger.

So to Facebook I went and found him quickly enough. Actually, about *six* of him. All the same guy.

I know several people who have opened up multiple Facebook accounts due to email address changes, spam attacks, and other legit reasons. But six open accounts… that was a bit of a surprise.

I selected the most recently active of the accounts, sent a friend request, used Messenger to inquire about where Cory had found my driver's license, and sat back to wait.

I did not wait long. Cory quickly replied that he had found my stuff on the roadway close to the Cutthroat Lake turnoff. He had been riding his bike down from the pass and had seen the cards lying on the pavement.

What about the wallet, I asked, and the credit cards? No sign of those, he said, but he hadn't looked around, either.

I expressed my gratitude for his quick return of my belongings...

And then things started clicking.

Even though I had no recollection of handling my wallet Thursday afternoon, I know myself well enough to figure that when I changed clothes I had removed my wallet from my pocket and temporarily put it on top of Terry's car. When Terry drove 100 yards up to the Cutthroat turnoff to head us back to Winthrop, the thin little wallet had skittered off the roof of the Subaru and into the roadway, there to be run over by countless cars and trucks, until at some point the contents were flung hither and yon. And some of them found by biker Cory on his way down from the pass.

I still felt uneasy about Cory's story, though. Something seemed to be missing. He didn't have a Methow location listed on Facebook. The six profiles bothered me. Did he maybe steal my wallet from Terry's car?

And then... ping! He messaged me saying he was sending me photos.

That's never a good sign on Messenger. Am I right? Or am I right?

I was just about to block the newly-suspect Cory when the pictures came through.

And at this point in the story, I must digress. Bigly.

Two weeks prior, as I have previously recounted, a couple of buddies and I had spent the week in a dispersed camp off Cutthroat Creek. With the extended stay in the woods, we did not want to leave vehicles along the highway, so we had booked transportation to and from the trailhead with Methow Motion. That Friday afternoon, we had manhauled our gear up from Survey Camp on Cutthroat Creek to our scheduled pickup at the Cutthroat Lake turnoff.

Just before noon, as we sat on our Tupperware totes awaiting our minivan, we saw a cyclist working his way uphill in the midday heat.

Crazy dude, the three of us thought out loud in unison.

The crazy dude pulled up near me and stopped for a breather. And some conversation.

Quite a bit of conversation, really. Twenty minutes' worth. He learned a good deal about us and how we had spent our week. And we learned that he worked in the maintenance department at Sun Mountain Lodge. We learned about the various places he'd hiked in the area and that for most of the summer he was living out of his Airstream at Lone Fir Campground, just a mile or so below Cutthroat Creek.

But I failed to catch his name.

As we spoke, I had the strangest feeling that the encounter was not entirely random. Like this gentleman and I were bound to cross paths again, at the very least because I spend so much time on Cutthroat Creek and he spends so much time at Lone Fir.

So let's reel this in again.

Ping! The photos come through on Messenger... and what do you know? One of them is a selfie of Cory on his bike with Liberty Bell in the background.

Now I recognized him. The photo might well have been taken the afternoon that we spoke for twenty minutes at the Cutthroat Lake turnoff.

And this very same stranger, whom I had entertained, was the angel who found my driver's license lying in the roadway two weeks later.

He thought I looked familiar.

What are the odds?

Wonderstruck.

■

Lolita in Tehran

I saw the book lying on the shoulder of Highway 20.

The first time was on my way to Thriftway to get a sandwich for lunch. On the way back to The Iron Horse, I noticed the cover flapping in the wake of the car in front of me, just off the verge of grass by The Virginian's signboard.

I figured I knew how it got there. I had, after all, only recently lost my wallet by placing it on top of the car and then forgetting about it. More than likely, the book had suffered a similar fate.

I presumed that the owner would be by soon to pick it up.

Later that afternoon when I went to Ace to pick up camping supplies, the book was still there. On my way home from Ace, I again passed the flapping book in front of The Virginian. After another twenty yards I slowed to a stop.

Just days prior, a stranger had seen my driver's license and stopped to pick it up. Could I possibly return a similar favor? Granted, people don't usually leave their phone numbers or addresses in the books they read… but who knows?

At the very least, I could take it along for reading material during my upcoming week on Ross Lake.

In fact, maybe I was *meant* to read the book, whatever it was.

I put the Yaris in park and walked back along Highway 20 to retrieve the lost tome: Azar Nafisi's *Reading Lolita in Tehran*. The book's owner had apparently read about forty pages before losing it, and there were no bookmarks or writing on the flap.

I remember reading a review of the book when it was released in 2003. It did not strike me as good reading material then. That seemed immaterial now. Back in the Yaris, I threw the book in with my camping gear and made my preparations for Ross Lake that evening.

The next evening on Cat Island, I began reading Nafisi's memoir of her subversive encounter with literature. I continued to snatch moments throughout the week, absorbing, for the first time in quite awhile, another literature nerd's thoughts on various works of classic world literature.

I wouldn't say that my read was earth-shattering. It was more like a slow sunrise through a cloud-shrouded horizon, punctuated by periodic shafts of light. For example:

> Was it necessary to put this book on trial? I was somewhat taken aback. Did he want me to throw the book aside without so much as a word in its defense? Anyway, this is a good time for trials, I said, is it not?

For the past few weeks, I have been wondering what the next year holds for me. My life tends to follow a pattern of five-year "seasons." Next year will mark the end of my fifth year in the Methow Valley, and, if anything, the theme of this latest season has been "change." Very little has been settled; but I have been feeling like the stage has been set for a season of stability. What will fill this season?

I continued to mull this question over in my mind during my week on Ross Lake and talked about it at length with my hiking buddy, The Shy Pilot. *Reading Lolita in Tehran* struck me as a running commentary on my thoughts and discussions.

Then, on the final evening of the week, as we were prepping dinner in the privacy of our camp at May Creek, a couple wandered down from the East Bank Trail. They had come from the stock camp to get fresh water, bathe, and cook dinner. We invited them to use the beach at our camp rather than the far-less attractive boat dock. They gladly agreed and enjoyed the Golden Hour light.

After we finished our dinners separately, I wandered over to introduce myself and chat a little.

The chat turned into quite an interesting conversation. Gail and Jim Scott traveled from Abbotsford, B.C., to take the East Bank Trail to the summit of Desolation Peak… which they had bagged that afternoon, and they were now on their way back to the trailhead.

Gail and Jim have finished writing their first novel and submitted it to a publisher just before leaving for the hike.

I mentioned that I am also a publisher.

We then talked at length of literature and theology, and the interplay of faith and culture. Jim and I reviewed our histories in publishing.

Did I mention that their novel is about the interesting and unexpected conversations that strangers have in the backcountry?

The next morning, after packing up my camp, I had a few minutes of quiet to sit on the May Creek beach and reflect on the week's reading and conversations.

How strange to spend the last four years immersed in art and literature and still somehow lose track of the fact that literature is both my passion and my calling.

How strange to rediscover that fact because of a book left on the top of someone's car and a serendipitous meeting on a wilderness beach.

How strange is this life? And how wonderful?

■

Meza

I apparently have a knack for discovering elegant cuisine on a restaurant's opening day.

Three years ago, that was the pub at Twisp Terrace Lodge; a couple weeks ago, on a soft-opening Saturday, the exceedingly pleasant surprise was Casey Peplow's Meza, boasting more than thirty beverages on tap and a *tapas*-inspired menu in the two-years-shuttered space that used to be Sixknot on Winthrop's boardwalk. (Yes, Sixknot became a Covid casualty!)

Of course, the discovery was awfully easy this time as Meza is right next door to The Iron Horse. We've been watching the prep for opening some time now, and I've had the inside skinny from Sixknot's John Sinclair, who has had a hand in bringing Meza to the space.

I have to say I can't be happier to have such a fine food venue alongside my place of business. Not only is the menu unique—you won't find these particular Spanish and Mediterranean influences offered elsewhere in the Valley—the preparation and presentation make you aware that this isn't just food, something to be consumed to merely satisfy your daily caloric intake requirements. No. It's cuisine.

After several visits I've had nearly everything on the menu, and it's all excellent. Highlights include the Spanish cheeses and meats on the Mezze plate; the sweet potato puree and garlic Greek yogurt that accompany several dishes; and the seasoned meatballs.

But gosh—have you ever had Romesco? It's a Spanish dipping sauce that looks much like a red pepper hummus; but the primary ingredients are tomato, garlic, and nuts (rather than garbanzos), and at Meza it comes as an accompaniment to several of the small plates. Look for it. It's out of this world!

And it's all served in that really cozy and appealing space that John designed for Sixknot. Casey has updated the wall treatments for a more European look; but that has only enhanced what Sixknot began. In just two weeks, Meza has become my favorite hangout spot.

Sometimes I just have to pinch myself at my good fortune.

■

Deadfall

I spent nearly sixty years preparing for the moment.

On the way out to clear the brush from the Early Winters ford on the Peace Trail, Kaileah Akker and I stopped to remove debris from a section that Mike Liu had bucked a week prior. The corpses of several large snags had crisscrossed the trail, and now they had been bisected, with the excised logs rolled up along the skirts of the trail.

As Kaileah and I heaved chunks of bark and limbs out of the path, another massive widowmaker towering over us sighed and creaked in the breeze.

Just a couple miles or so distant, a heaving thunderstorm was sending boulders coursing over Dead Horse Point on the Harts Pass road, and hail was battering Mazama; the thunder would roll just beyond Silver Star throughout the afternoon.

But here on the upper Early Winters, the sun was peeking out between the clouds. Unbeknownst to me, Mike Liu's family was enjoying a dip in the Cutthroat Cascades alongside Survey Camp. The breeze was light, just enough to make this old snag conversational but not threatening. I crossed the gully and laid my hands on its bare bole. In the moment, it felt like one of Tolkien's old Ents.

On down the path we went, and fifteen minutes later we laid our packs at the ford. After some discussion, we decided exactly where the clearing of the ford would commence, and we set to work with saws and hand-pruners. The near bank was cleared quickly, and then for the next ninety minutes we hacked away at the flood-plain alder densely packed on the opposite bank.

While we sat on the newly cleared opposite landing for a rest, I pondered three snags that towered over the stream bank facing us. A log footbridge would be so advantageous at this ford in the flood season… if only one of those trees could be persuaded to fall across the creek. The one to the left leaned entirely the wrong way and would likely fall parallel to the streambed. The middle one was quite distant, and who knows which direction it would fall?

But the one to the right… It had potential. It was right at the creek's edge and just a few feet away from the downstream trail. Perhaps it would one day do us a favor and cross Early Winters gracefully.

We returned to work and within another hour had cleared the alder grove, actually locating the historic Early Winters trailbed through it in the process and connecting the downstream portion of the trail with the upper section of the trail Jason Suter and I had located two years prior. We saddled up our gear and retraced our steps to the ford for a final cleanup. I snapped a photo of Kaileah in the clearing on the far bank, just to put the work in perspective.

She then waded into the stream to join me in grabbing debris and tossing it aside. We were both facing the center of the stream, she on the far side and I with my back to the near bank.

Over the babbling of the Early Winters, I heard a rustling in the brush behind me and to my left. I turned to see what it might be, expecting a bear. Long branches of scrub alder were thrashing right at the stream's edge; and then a crack, and in the blur above the lenses of my glasses I perceived the bole of that enormous dead fir heading directly toward where I was standing.

I had time to think, "It's probably going to miss me, but I'm taking no chances!" and spun to my right, flinging myself to the red-granite gravel beach. I had no time to alert Kaileah. All she heard was me hitting the ground.

The next either of us knew, that tree had fallen exactly across the ford we had just cleared. Less than two minutes had elapsed since I had taken Kaileah's photo in that exact spot. For ninety minutes we had labored in that widowmaker's path. For ten we had sat on that bank in silence and rested. For a couple of those, I had thought about that very tree falling and bridging the ford.

"If a tree falls in the forest and no one is there to hear it," it has been asked many times, "does it make a sound?"

Well, I was there to see this one fall. It nearly killed both Kaileah and me, but we emerged unscathed. As Kaileah texted me later in the day, "it's a wonder (we weren't) struck."

I honestly don't know what to make of the experience. But I do know I didn't hear a thing.

And the forest is awake.

Thingol and Melian

> 'Twas in a forest such as this that Thingol espied Melian and fell in love with her.

At least, if I were to stand spellbound for years, I would choose such a forest.

"Which forest?" you may well ask. "And who is Thingol?" you may better ask.

I'll get there.

For the last three summers I have been working on restoration of the Early Winters Trail from Lone Fir toward Washington Pass. Why? Because I have fallen in love with a waterfall. Willow Creek Falls, to be precise, the one you can see across the Early Winters basin from Highway 20 as you descend from Washington Pass.

Since I could find no documented trail to the foot of the falls, I decided to make one.

Starting from Lone Fir on the maintained official trail, which utilizes a portion of the historical Early Winters Trail (EWT), was the easy beginning. The EWT, in its heyday, extended from Jack Wilson's ranch at what is now Freestone all the way to a connection with the Cascade Crest Trail—later part of the Pacific Crest Trail and finally established as a National Scenic Trail in 1968.

By that time, the North Cascades Highway was well under way, the opening of which led to the demise of the EWT. Large portions of the lower trail were co-opted for the route of Highway 20, and the big switchback at Washington Pass obliterated the route below Liberty Bell.

Over time, the remaining trail, which was largely a pack animal route in origin and not frequently hiked in the first place, fell into disuse. Today, the only heavily traveled route in the area is the steep climber's trail used to access Silver Star and the Vasiliki Towers—and that trail merely bisects the EWT on its way across the drainage from highway to peaks.

So making the trail walkable from Cutthroat Creek to Willow Creek has been a chore, but a blessed one. I have spent countless hours out in those woods in solitude, as well as in the company of tremendous comrades who have also been bitten by the bug.

The stories behind the last three summers are many, and I have told them here and elsewhere; but by the end of August it was clear that the final trek to Willow Creek was going to be possible to close the season. I scheduled the hike for September 30 and invited my fellow trailworkers to join me.

I was aware that the trek would roughly coincide with the fiftieth anniversary of the formal opening of the North Cascades Highway. And the irony was not lost on me. But I did not expect to see detailed articles about the history of the pass in the September 21 edition of the *Methow Valley News*.

And I really didn't expect to find quotes in Marcy Stamper's articles from living crew members who had actually worked on the survey crews for the highway—men who had walked and packed animals on the trail that I have been reclaiming. I contacted Don Nelson and Marcy Stamper and asked them to get me in touch with Tom Graves and Chuck McCallum.

On Tuesday, Tom Graves walked into The Iron Horse and pulled up a stool to chat. He's 93 now but still sharp as a tack. In 1962, he was the packer for the survey crew camped at Willow Creek. At the end of our conversation, he mentioned finding large black crystals on the trail near Willow Creek and at the survey camp. He thinks he still has them packed away in a box somewhere.

On Wednesday, I went out to do some final trail prep with Dave Chase. He's a fairly recent full-time Methow Valley resident but has been visiting regularly since he was a teenager. Wednesday was the first time I have really had a chance to talk with him. Back in the early '70s, not long after the opening of the pass, his family would camp at Early Winters. They befriended an older couple who had been summer camping at Early Winters for decades… and they also reported finding black crystals in the area. At some point they gave Dave's parents samples of minerals from Early Winters and Blewett Pass, including those black crystals. Dave also believes he has those rusty tins sitting on a shelf somewhere. They are probably either rutilated quartz or tourmaline.

On Thursday, Chuck McCallum called. In 1962, the summer I was born, he had been a member of the four-man survey crew camped at Cutthroat Creek—where earlier this summer, I and two of my college buddies spent four days. Bob George was the crew boss that summer of 1962, and teams worked in fourteen-day rotations of ten days' work on the survey and four days off downstream. So he travelled the eight miles from Early Winters to Cutthroat Creek many, many times that summer. He recalls that Lone Fir was a hunter's camp at that time, with Jack Wilson's cabin downstream from there a couple miles. At the conclusion of the summer, he joined his grandfather and other dignitaries on a horseback camping trip all the way up the EWT, past Willow Creek and beyond, to preview the route of the highway.

What a prelude for Friday.

After ninety minutes of hiking, our party of four came to the end of the section of the EWT previously brushed and flagged. At the conclusion of a sweaty August day in 2020, Jason Suter and I had stood at the edge of a tangled gully nearly half a mile below Willow Creek and could no longer locate the overgrown trailbed. We had retreated with our tails between our legs, as I thought the going would likely deteriorate from there. But I didn't know it would be another two years before I would be back at that spot.

In those intervening two years, the preliminary work of brushing and flagging paid off big time. Since then, some unknown backcountry whiz has noticed that the section of the EWT from the Vasiliki Trail across the Burgundy Creek floodplain and beyond has been opened up; and that fellow explorer has blazed the route of the trailbed with parallel saw marks on trees that have fallen across the trail.

Covering the last half mile to Early Winters Creek was not nearly the chore on Friday that I expected it to be, thanks to that explorer!

And the trail is actually in better shape there than it is in the area around Burgundy Creek.

Which brings me, finally, to Thingol.

The forest around Willow Creek is stunning. As with the rest of the watershed above the Silver Star carpark, it has never burned, nor has it been logged. It is a primitive forest, as new as it always has been over the centuries. Here the Early Winters valley floor is broad and flat, and the forest suffers neither from rainforest-like denseness, as it does in places further downvalley, nor from excessive windfall. The forest is healthy. Sunlight filters down to the forest floor everywhere, and the boles of the trees are well spaced so that you can see for hundreds of yards through them in all directions. Sunlight blazes off foliage. Nowhere does the brush grow into thickets.

I have always been a fan of J.R.R. Tolkien's love of nature and the way in which he writes about it in *The Hobbit*, *The Lord of the Rings*, *The Silmarillion*, and the vast remainder of his body of work.

Thingol features in one of the seminal storylines of Tolkien's backstory mythology. The Elf Lord wandered in a forest once in the early days of the world, and there encountered the goddess Melian. I imagine it must have been a forest much like that near Willow Creek, though I suppose the trees were grander.

After returning from the hike to Willow Creek, I sat down to watch the latest episode of *The Rings of Power* on Amazon Prime. I really didn't expect to enjoy it as much as I did; but the dialogue between the Elf Galadriel and the Uruk Adar reminded me so much of what I love about Tolkien's work; and while I was watching the rest of the program, some themes that have been percolating in my head for my upcoming novel *Early Winters* started to boil. At the conclusion of the program, I sat down at the computer to revisit the closing paragraphs of the novel, which were among the first parts of the manuscript that I drafted.

I had forgotten that I had written these words more than two years ago:

> We do not get "happy endings" in this life; but we may get "happy turnings," what Tolkien called "eucatastrophe," which offer a shadow of or homage to true salvation. But even these bend sad or bittersweet as various passings occur. Tolkien believed that, too; or have you not read "The Grey Havens"?
>
> So we embrace the seasons as they come. Sometimes the beauty of spring catches us unawares; sometimes we linger in a vernal paradise; we may thrill to the strange magic of the Indian summer in a Methow October; and sometimes it's nothing but early winters.

Oh, but such happy turnings these four days. So much serendipity in a week that has brought so many threads of the last three years together in such a satisfying way. The strange magic of the Indian summer. Thrilling.

Wonderstruck.

Leen

Danbert Nobacon was nowhere to be found.

I had stopped by the Cinema on a snowy evening to chat a bit and get my copy of Chumbawamba's *Tubthumper* autographed. The band's frontman Danbert clerks The Barnyard some evenings, and I was hoping to catch him idle between screenings.

Upon walking through the door, I easily discerned that I had, indeed, caught The Barnyard between screenings. The lobby was empty.

Because the lobby was empty, I could also easily see that the figure at the far end of the bar was not Danbert.

My immediate impulse was to turn and leave, mission unaccomplished. I nonetheless strode forward and asked if Danbert happened to be in. No, of course not. If he had been, I'd have seen him. There would be nowhere else for Danbert to be but visible.

As I turned to leave, I said, "Well, I only dropped in to talk with Danbert. Not that I wouldn't enjoy talking with you, too, but you're not Danbert. Have a nice evening."

And as I was halfway through the door, it occurred to me: "Why *not* talk to whoever it was who was not Danbert?" Times such as these and all. Sometimes the unexpected is exactly what we need.

And so I returned to the lobby.

And I met Leen, raised in the Valley but only recently returned after an extended sojourn on "the Coast," as locals refer to anywhere west of the Cascades. While there she had completed her studies in Cinema and Social Services at the University of Washington (where twenty-five years earlier I had also studied Cinema) and worked for a number of years in the latter field, including a stint with DSHS. She is again, now, on home ground. Which includes The Barnyard.

Leen and I shared an extraordinarily pleasant chat. In a brief space, we covered a digest of personal histories, a shared love of the cinema, and highlights of recent releases like *The Banshees of Inisherin*, favorite films like *Babette's Feast* and *Ghost Story*, and my own foray into filmmaking, *Who Shall Stand*. Since the popcorn machine cleaning schedule took precedence, we terminated our discussion and I took my pleasant leave.

On the drive home, I had occasion to mull over the stories of *The Fewkes Legacy*, a literary cycle of which the *Who Shall Stand* screenplay renders the second part. My novel *West of the Gospel* is the fourth segment in the cycle. And then, out of nowhere, as I approached Wolf Creek Road and the moonlight played on the snow-drifted alfalfa fields, the opening words of the as-yet-unwritten third tale, *The Boar's Nest*, came to me: "Sideways blew the snow, and Thomas Fewkes with it."

I made sure to write that down when I arrived home. Inspiration of a certain kind can be readily lost amidst the bustle of everyday life.

And then Misuk and I sat down to watch a documentary about the seven years it took for Leonard Cohen to write "Hallelujah." During the film, Cohen's rabbi talked about the theological underpinnings of Cohen's art, and the necessary wait for the spirit of inspiration to come, and the patience involved in the listening.

Hallelujah, indeed.

I have been waiting twenty-five years for the opening words of *The Boar's Nest*. And they came because of the path I chose in the doorway of The Barnyard after stopping by the cinema on a snowy evening.

Frost would be intrigued. So would Isak Dinesen, the author behind *Babette's Feast*. Something of a Ghost Story, indeed. A holy Ghost Story. A Holy Ghost story? Capital.

And then these words in my email inbox this morning from filmmaker and friend Cris Krusen:

> What moves you to tenderness? To tears? What softens the sharp edges of your heart? Follow those impulses. ... Don't brush those encounters aside or hurry past. If the welcome mat is out for you, you will surely do well to wipe your feet and sit a while with your hosts. And who knows... maybe catch a piece of heaven in the bargain.

Wonderstruck.

■

Beast Mode

…so that's when I went off on the bear.

For the last two years, we've been harassed by brown bears at our Twin Lakes home outside Winthrop. The 2021 Cedar Fire to our west burned tens of thousands of acres and destroyed a good deal of animal habitat.

Last spring, a small cinnamon-colored and displaced yearling discovered the green goodness of our watered yard, wallowing on the fresh-cut lawn, enjoying long drinks from the birdbaths, and curling up for naps in the sunshine. Aside from the first time getting at our trash (we didn't repeat that mistake) he was pretty placid, if habitual. The first time I spotted him (while mowing the lawn!), I ended up treeing him—and Fish & Wildlife had to come out and paintball him out of the tree.

This year, though, well… we have had at least four different bears on the property and they have been destructive—thrashing the barbecue, ripping down bird feeders, dumping the birdbaths. You name it. One of the devils even had the gall to paw at the sliding glass door on Misuk's office… while Misuk was standing just three feet away, watching. And this year when we call Fish & Wildlife… well, join the party. The whole area is dealing with the bear invasion. We're pretty much on our own to cope.

So, this year, coping has pretty much included abandoning any hope of outdoor relaxation. We don't dare leave anything portable and thrashable outside, and we can't imagine sitting outside and possibly falling asleep.

And don't even talk about fences. Our yard is already lined with eight-foot deer fence, and the bears just climb trees to get over. The smaller ones can even squeeze through gaps not much bigger than one foot square.

Yesterday afternoon I rose from the couch and turned toward the kitchen to put dinner in the oven... and there, rumbling slowly past the dining room slider, was the biggest bear to date. He looked like Gentle Ben, if you remember that TV show.

So that's when I went off on the bear.

Without much thinking (and hence shouting a choice expletive) I dashed over to the door and peeked through to make sure the bear hadn't stopped at the end of the deck. Then I quickly slid open the glass and reached for the BB rifle I have kept handy for just such an opportunity.

As I rushed the bear and pumped the rifle, the startled bear—about twenty feet away and headed for a cuddle on the lawn—instantly spooked and dashed toward the fence line, quickly scuttling up the one-hundred-foot ponderosa which abuts the fence.

Thanks to some Boy Scout be-prepared target practice (and observation during last year's Fish & Wildlife visit) I knew exactly what to do. Before the big ol' black could get too high in the tree, I peppered the trunk (and yes, that's a pretty slooooow pepper) just above the bear's head with BB shot. Thinking that going higher might be a bad idea and still being within reach of a very tall man, the bear thought better of prolonging his visit and launched himself over the fence from his stance in the tree.

Another couple of shots over his head from my trusty Daisy, and he was well on his way to harass some other poor folks' property.

Back inside, listening to the adrenaline thump in my carotid, I was astonished at the rapidity of both my ire and my movements.

Perhaps it was because I had just been watching a Seahawks film on the 2013 Super Bowl season.

All fired up, you know: The Legion of Boom. Marshawn Lynch.

Beast Mode. Yeah.

■

In Memory Of

What inspires me to write? Things that intrigue me.

And once I decide to write, I most often learn a great deal, much more than I knew when I was first intrigued. I suppose that's one of the reasons I write. I know that if I pursue the things that intrigue me, I am bound to open my mind and heart to the unknown.

For several years now, I have been driving Twin Lakes Road daily, going back and forth between my home at Twin Lakes' Sun Mountain Ranch Club and The Iron Horse in Winthrop.

Toward the end of the long open curve east of the Wolf Creek Road fork, a roadside memorial has long clung to the bitterbrush hillside near the Winthrop Trail gate. A hand-lettered sign there reads "In loving memory of Josh and Rachel—you will be in our hearts always."

For years, three of every four seasons have seen a steady resupply of fresh-cut flowers decorating the sign. A large jug has sat nearby to help keep the blossoms watered.

As a person who knows first-hand the tragic loss of a loved one at far too young an age, I have often mentally remarked on the faithfulness of the tribute and wondered how long that has been going on.

I also know, from first-hand experience, that remembrance does not go on indefinitely. There are limits. The living, after all, keep living and finding other things that demand attention—and remembrance. One cannot observe them all.

This year along Twin Lakes Road, things have changed. Not only have the fresh flowers disappeared, the state-installed roadside signage is also noticeably deteriorating. The large panel on the signpost reads, "PLEASE DON'T DRINK AND DRIVE." That sign is pre-printed: mass-produced, a sad fact of necessity. It does not deteriorate.

Below that, a smaller second panel starts with, "IN MEMORY OF." That initial legend is also mass-produced; but following that, the blank spot in the mass-produced sign is filled with one-off applique lettering. This one used to list the full names of Rachel and Josh, but time, summer heat, and snowplow debris have flaked most of the lettering away.

Now, for my part, in the wake of my late wife's death, I learned that I am incapable of keeping promises based on emotion and attachment—even, yes, profound and sacrificial love.

The stories behind that realization must wait for another day to tell; but it has been on my mind this summer as my daily trips past Josh and Rachel's memorials have brought daily reminders that I am not alone in my failure to follow through on good intentions.

Intrigued, I finally thought, "This is something I need to write about."

Now, the art of literature is, in part, one of fitting form to subject. An idea that is a good fit for haiku, for instance, will not stretch to a novel. The reverse is just as true.

So a poem is almost always about the rigorous choice of forms and words—choosing which to use, which to leave unused, which to substitute for better words, even which to trim, precious though they be.

What I did not expect, when deciding to write a poem about Josh and Rachel, was how *many* words I would have to trim. The things I learned when diving down their particular rabbit hole would be enough to fill a book.

The roadside "Don't Drink and Drive" signage, for instance. Since Twin Lakes Road is an Okanogan County road, I presumed the sign must have been erected by the County. But I could find no information about any County program. At the state level, though, such signs are administered by Washington State's Department of Transportation.

The requirements for posting are copious and strict. The memorial signs can only be posted in cases where the driver causing the fatality is convicted for homicide due to driving under the influence or when toxicology reports demonstrate that the driver also died while intoxicated. Signage can only be requested by an immediate family member or with written permission by the family. The signage must be paid for by the requesting party. So I learned that either a conviction was obtained in Rachel's and Josh's deaths or that the driver causing the accident also died.

But when did the accident happen? While I waited for a reply to my query of WSDOT, I turned to the Internet.

A search of *Methow Valley News* digital archives came up empty. This led me to believe that the memorials have been there much longer than I expected. I have only lived in the

Methow for five years, and they must have already been quite old when I arrived.

I cast my net wider. I'm pretty good with Internet research, but finding further details armed only with first names, a road name, and a town was a challenge. After several hours of searching, I finally hit on a combination that yielded a single reference.

Late in 1997, the Spokane *Spokesman-Review* ran a guest column by Debbie Kalmbach about the memorial on Twin Lakes Road. The piece confirmed what I already knew and suspected: the victims' first names, the location of the accident, and that it was a result of DUI. But now I had three more crucial pieces of information: the name of someone who knew more about the memorial than I did; a date for the deaths, August 16, 1997; and the fact that Josh and Rachel had been passengers in the single-car incident, in which both the surviving eighteen-year-old driver and a twenty-three-year-old alcohol supplier had been charged.

To learn more, I tracked down Debbie Kalmbach. The name was familiar, so I thought I might have run across it on Facebook at some point. Sure enough, there she was: and who should be on our mutual friends list but my very own wife, Misuk Ko? Deb lived in the Valley until recently and had worked at Misuk's dentist's office. Small and bizarre world. From Facebook I culled the URL for Deb's life-coaching website and visited it to fire off a query about Josh and Rachel's surnames.

While I waited for that reply, I pored over an enlarged photo of the battered DOT sign to try to decipher the surnames.

Only three consecutive letters remained of Rachel's: AND. Josh's was more sketchy, with what looked like A_KIS_ON, or perhaps just KIS_ON, as I was unsure whether the A was part of "Joshua." My stabs at surnames that fit the remaining letters were coming up blank on Internet searches.

Deb did not take long to reply, however. To her recollection, the teens' names were Rachel Sandy and Josh Atkinson. Armed with these full names and the date of the accident that Deb reported, I was then able to email Don Nelson at *Methow Valley News* and ask him to search the paper archives to confirm details. He reported that the names were Rachel Sandy and Joshua Atkisson—which made more sense of the tattered letters than Atkinson and explained why further searches on Atkinson were coming up empty.

Now my Googling for Atkisson hit directly on obituaries, death reports, and memorial marker data at Beaver Creek Cemetery. Josh was just fifteen and died August 15, 1997, in Wenatchee. Rachel Sandy was sixteen and died the following day.

For twenty-five years, those keeping the memorial kept it well. I don't know if that total of years was significant, but apparently it finally felt like enough for whoever was keeping it. I'm quite sure the pain of loss was still there, but the moving on had finally become visible.

And in the middle of the following summer—this year, on July 18—another car with four teenagers rolled on Twisp River Road, just five miles distant as the crow flies. Two more hospitalizations, one more death at the scene: Kierra Reichert, age nineteen. The memorial service was held on August 12 at the Red Barn in Winthrop. I think almost everyone in Winthrop was there.

And I have to wonder what those who had been keeping Josh and Rachel's memorial for twenty-five years must have been thinking.

So tell me—what words are worth losing when trying to write a poem about such loss and tragedy?

Which words are worth keeping?

■

Nobacon

Yes, I know a man named Danbert Nobacon.

For those who do not know Danbert, this "singer, songwriter, comedian, and 'freak music legend'" was "a founding member of the anarchist punk rock band Chumbawamba." Unlike many embellished promotional mini-biographies, this one happens to be fully true.

Also true: "He loves children and animals."

Among other gigs that occupy his time, Danbert bartends and popper-tends at The Barnyard Cinema in Winthrop. He is also a band performer, actor, director, stage manager, playwright, promoter, producer, sound designer, light technician, and set designer at The Merc Playhouse in Twisp, doubling up his role as co-director of The Liberty Bell Drama Company for the Methow Valley School District.

He is also a loving father.

Since I moved to the Methow, I have had occasion to cross paths with Danbert, frequenting as I do some of the same environs as does he, as well as sharing several close acquaintances.

When I stumbled across a CD of *Tubthumper* Chumbawamba's seminal album (which contains their signature hit "Tubthumping") on a shelf in our living room, I thought it was finally time to talk at length with Danbert about his art.

The pretext was to ask him to autograph the disc for me!

So when Danbert graciously stopped by The Iron Horse one slow afternoon this summer, I was able to learn a great deal more about the band's history, the origin of Danbert's moniker (that's his story to tell), and his history in the Methow.

But the most fascinating thing I learned was that, amongst all his other artistic pursuits, he had also authored a teen novel, *3 Dead Princes*, illustrated by gonzo filmmaker Alex Cox and carrying endorsements from the likes of Iggy Pop. Rowr!

I am writing this today because last night, as the final indulgence of celebrating my sixty-first birthday, I finished reading *3 Dead Princes*. What a gift!

Now, I have often confessed that I am perhaps the least well-read writer on the planet. And in recent decades, the vast majority of the reading that I have done has been non-fiction. The reasons?

Well, first, I really can't read poetry, *per se*. Though that has been my preferred form of expression for the last decade, I take about six months to work my way through a typical volume of poetry. What I do with poetry is digest it, and slowly.

Second, I honestly can't remember the last time a work of fiction absolutely delighted me. It may have been decades ago, the first time I read Booth Tarkington's *Kate Fennigate*. Or *Little Orvie*. I think I must get too distracted while reading most fiction to actually enjoy it.

But, wow. Several times, *3 Dead Princes* caused me to exclaim out loud in joy as I read. Danbert's "Anarchist Fairy Tale" exploration of science, religion, culture, and familial bonds exhibits such creative engagement with language (and hope) that it can't help but make me smile. I am gobsmacked.

The book closes as follows:

> If we let it, wonder conquers darkness every time.

■

Early Winters

Winter actually comes late to the Methow Valley this year…

But on July 18, 1999, the New York Yankees hosted "Yogi Berra Days," a celebration of the legend's first return to Yankee Stadium in fourteen years following a prolonged feud with Yankees owner George Steinbrenner.

The ceremonial first pitch was thrown to Berra by former Yankee pitcher Don Larsen. In 1956, the two had worked together to throw the only perfect game in World Series history, to win it all.

On the mound on July 18, 1999, was David Cone… who also proceeded to throw a perfect game. Now, what are the odds of that?

The somewhat younger Yankee legend Derek Jeter has said about that day, "I believe there are ghosts in Yankee Stadium… The strangest things happen there."

◼

November 18, 2023. I'm behind the counter at The Iron Horse in Winthrop, Washington. I've had most of the week off and have spent it writing the opening pages of my new novel, *Early Winters*. The setting of the story is, as you might guess if you know the area, the Early Winters Creek drainage up toward Washington Pass. I have been doing the background research for the story for three years, and this week, conditions conspired to break things loose and allow me to start the actual writing.

It's a slow day at the store. All told, we'll have about ten customers. So it's easy to engage in quiet chatter with the tourists.

One couple a few years older than I come into the shop and are particularly taken with The Iron Horse's collection of old-school outdoor gear, hats, and wrought iron.

"Where are you folks visiting from?" I use my standard query for further engagement.

"Oh, just from Omak," the man says.

"You're very familiar with the area, then."

"Yes," he says. "I even lived over here as a boy."

"Where at?" I ask.

"Early Winters," he says. "My dad was the Forest Service ranger there."

Imagine that. The very week I begin writing *Early Winters*, and the first day I'm back in the store, one of the few customers that will be in the shop actually grew up at Early Winters. I am naturally taken aback.

"Really?" I remark. "Then your dad must have known Jack Wilson." The latter established the Early Winters and Freestone resorts, and ran pack trains up Robinson Creek, the upper Methow River, and Early Winters Creek. Wilson is an enormous part of the backstory to *Early Winters*.

"Oh, yes," the man said. "I'm named after Wilson. And my mom painted the portrait of Jack that used to hang in Freestone Inn."

And so it was I met Wilson Woolschlager, son of Ranger Hawley Lee Woolschlager, who just passed away in June of this year.

What do you think Derek Jeter would have to say about Early Winters?

■

Methow's Bombadil

> The wind puffed out. The leaves hung silently again on stiff branches. There was another burst of song, and then suddenly, hopping and dancing along the path, there appeared above the reeds an old battered hat with a tall crown and a long blue feather stuck in the band. With another hop and a bound there came into view a man, or so it seemed. At any rate he was too large and heavy for a Hobbit, if not quite tall enough for one of the Big People, though he made noise enough for one, slumping along with great yellow boots on his thick legs, and charging through grass and rushes like a cow going down to drink. He had a blue coat and a long brown beard; his eyes were blue and bright, and his face was red as a ripe apple but creased into a hundred wrinkles of laughter.

No, I did not write that. The words are Tolkien's description of Frodo and Sam's first encounter with Tom Bombadil in *The Lord of the Rings*.

Who (or what) is Tom Bombadil? That's not the subject of this essay, but in short he's an otherworldly creature who is neither overly concerned with nor controlled by the events and conditions of the physical world. He simply occupies it. Once you encounter Tom Bombadil, you know you've been in the presence of something extraordinary—something the likes of which you shall not likely encounter again.

On Friday, September 13, I met Kate and Cary Therriault at the Lone Fir Campground for a guided tour of the historic Early Winters Trail. Earlier in the summer, Kate had placed the winning bid for the tour at the Public School Funding Alliance silent auction fundraiser hosted by Arrowleaf Bistro. After several false starts, Kate and I finally managed to coordinate our schedules so I could make good on the winning bid. Kate and Cary brought Jane Gilbertsen along for the hike.

At one time, the Early Winters Trail followed Early Winters Creek from what is now Freestone Inn up and over Washington Pass and down to Rainy Pass. The trail was essentially built and maintained by Jack Wilson for his personal use as a trapper, to ferry backcountry clients via pack train, and to serve as access for his contracts to construct trail for the Cascade Crest and Pacific Crest trails.

Once Wilson's campaign to use the Early Winters drainage for construction of the North Cascades Highway came to fruition, the trail fell into disuse. Miles of it disappeared under SR 20's asphalt, and the trail's original purpose simply ceased to be.

By the 1990s, only a couple of trail sections were still maintained by the USFS—one piece accessed from Klipchuck Campground and the other at Lone Fir.

The Lone Fir section was turned into a loop trail, with the access link between the campground and the bottom of the loop paved and lined with interpretive signage designed by Laura Bitzes Thomas during her time with the USFS. Two log bridges were put across Early Winters, and numerous smaller bridges and boardwalks were constructed to span flooding spring tributaries and troublesome marshes.

A years-long closure of Lone Fir, however, due to a pine bark beetle infestation, led to neglect of the loop trail. Many of the boardwalks and bridges fell into disrepair. At the present time, two of the major bridges have been entirely dismantled and removed by the USFS, and while the trail is not officially closed it is certainly not accessible in the way that it was designed. Just 200 yards from the trailhead, the paved path tumbles into a 50-foot-wide spring-runoff chasm.

So the trail is less-frequented now than it usually is. Already a well-kept secret featuring an old-growth forest full of multi-season wildflowers and fungi, it's the last place you would expect to simply bump into an acquaintance.

Though you wouldn't be surprised to bump into Tom Bombadil. It's that kind of place.

During the outward leg of our trail tour, in conversation with Kate, Jane mentioned having bumped into local legend and naturalist Dana Visalli on a trail up at Harts Pass. I wasn't part of that conversation, so I waited until we were straddling Early Winters Creek on the loop trail's upper bridge to follow up on Jane's mention of Dana.

I was delighted to learn that Kate and Cary were already familiar with the Methow Valley Authors Library at Casia Lodge, and that they had already visited. I shared with Jane that the library holds a complete collection of Dana's *Methow Naturalist*, a quarterly journal which includes the writing of dozens of local outdoors enthusiasts.

We all lamented that Dana intends to sunset the publication in the not-too-distant future.

On our return to our cars, we stopped to chat at the junction of the loop trail with the paved interpretive trail, and I took a couple group photos.

As we were preparing to depart, the wind puffed out. And then suddenly, hopping and dancing along the path, there came into view a man, or so it seemed. At any rate he was too large and heavy for a Hobbit, if not quite tall enough for one of the Big People, though he made noise enough for one, clumping along with great brown boots on his thick, bare legs, and charging down the path like a cow elk going down to drink. He wore a threadbare t-shirt and drab shorts; his eyes were blue and bright, and his grizzled face was red as a ripe apple but creased into a hundred wrinkles of laughter.

It was not Tom Bombadil… but it *was* Dana Visalli.

"It's as if we conjured him by speaking his name!" whispered Kate.

Jane and Dana, of course, knew each other—and Jane introduced Cary and Kate.

Dana explained that he was conducting his annual survey of valley fungi, and we offered that he would certainly find plenty of samples once he left the asphalt and entered the loop trail.

"Wonderful!" he exclaimed. "I've never been on this trail before."

Astounding. How could it possibly be that Dana Visalli, of all people, had never been on the Lone Fir leg of the Early Winters Trail? A well-kept secret indeed!

And how strange and fitting that the first local person I should encounter on the Early Winters Trail—over five years, dozens of visits, and hundreds of hours—should be Dana Visalli, on his first visit to the trail!

It might as well have *been* Tom Bombadil.

Wonderstruck.

Acknowledgements

There is no timeline for grief, but for me the two years following Jenn's tragic and magical passing were the crucible. I am indebted to those who were closest to me throughout my renaissance of joy:

- My oldest friend, Stephanie Cortes, always a trusted companion, who helped talk me through Jenn's hospice decline and beyond;
- My sister, Elane Rosok, who has always understood me, even when she tormented me as a child;
- Peter Alford, whose own life was in great flux as he encountered the closing months of mine and Jenn's, and who talked long and weekly with me for many years following Jenn's death;
- Fellow high school alumnus Denise Driscoll, who re-entered my life at just the right time to help get both my physical and spiritual bodies back in shape;
- College roommate John Adami, who has always seemed to have his forefinger on my spiritual pulse and re-enter my life at just the right times;

- Kaileah Akker, whose youthful energy and spiritual sensitivity have been invaluable in my journey on the eastern slope of the Cascades;
- Subhaga Crystal Bacon, whose friendship has encouraged a six-year outpouring of poetry and prose, and provided the final nudge to collect these essays;
- and most of all, my wife, Misuk Ko, whose keen questions and close reading of my essays have taught me that I do not need to say (or write) everything that passes through my mind… just the stuff that really matters.

www.ingramcontent.com/pod-product-compliance
Lightning Source LLC
Chambersburg PA
CBHW020355170426
43200CB00005B/178